The Waiting Room

STORIES OF

GETTING TO THE OTHER
SIDE OF THROUGH

The Waiting Room

VISIONARY AUTHOR

DEBBIE LESEAN

The Waiting Room

Manuscript editing
Georgina Chong You

Book Creation and Design
Ellese & Co Creative
www.elleseandco.com

ISBN: 978-1-7367808-7-9

Printed in the United States of America

Foreword

There are times when God says jump, but we have no idea what awaits us. We know in our hearts that He will work everything out for our good. However, the thoughts in our minds can begin to encourage us to second guess the most powerful being. Our reality has zero to do with what we see but all to do with what we believe. To see success in her reality, she must see success in her mind's eye.

As a woman prepares for the next phase in life, she sometimes finds herself in a Waiting Room. The Waiting Room can sometimes be the scariest because people may never know how long they have to be there. Some moments may even leave a person worried that they may miss out on their next appointment because this stage of life is taking longer than expected.

The women in this anthology realized there was beauty in their Waiting Room experience. Although they may not know what is next, their belief that something more significant is coming prepares them to have their preparation meet opportunity, resulting in God-sized success.

As a mental health expert, I chose this path in life because I had my own Waiting Room experience. Trauma had me rushing to Urgent Care because I felt like I could no longer handle the stressors of day-to-day life. I could no longer ignore the pain I felt because of broken relationships as a result of of being exposed to sexual experiences when I was three years old. Or the negative impact being obese at age thirteen had on my self-esteem. Also, I could not forget how being sexually assaulted at age sixteen made me feel. I found myself overcome with emotional pain, so I chose death when life became too overwhelming. Three seconds before I could put the poisonous concoction I had created into my mouth, my dad knocked down the door and served as CPR to my life. This moment is when my Waiting Room experience started.

I had to go through a process of meeting with my life's nurse (therapist) to uncover the negative core beliefs I subscribed to so I could make sense of life. I had to acknowledge my thoughts of "I am not good enough," "I am invisible," "I am ugly," "I am not enough," and many more that did not serve as a positive influence on my wellbeing. Once I recognized these negative thoughts, I began to hate how they made me feel so I made a change. This change started with me acknowledging the truth, I am the only Mylira in this world, and my story is not supposed to resemble someone else. This gave me permission to learn the me outside of the world's standards and fall in love with myself without conditions. This acknowledgment allowed me to embrace my differences. As I waited in my Waiting Room for my circumstances to change, I began to reflect on the unique qualities I brought to the tables and rooms I frequent. This allowed me to understand the purpose I was created to fulfill.

The Waiting Room allowed me to get into my quiet place to utilize my strengths and embrace my weaknesses without judging myself. When a woman enters her Waiting Room experience, others cannot go with her because it is where she gathers her thoughts and gets everything aligned before going to see the doctor (God). During this period, a woman must understand the things that come to her easily with the least resistance because these are her strengths. Furthermore, those things that serve as a challenge create space for genuine connections. The women in this project allowed for their sisters' stories to bring a strength that she alone may not have had. However, without the Waiting Room experience, this connection may not have been fully appreciated. In this space, women can become comfortable with being their authentic selves because they now know they are not alone.

I am currently in my personal Waiting Room. I used to always tell myself, "My soul's purpose is so big; I'm just waiting for my flesh to catch up." So, I jumped. I put in my resignation from my stable job and now waiting for God to reveal to me his plans. With no consistent money flowing in or clear vision of what's next can truly be a scary place to find oneself in. I have been the breadwinner for my family and now the once guaranteed resources are no longer assured. It's easy to question where "Where is God?" As much as I want to freak out, I know the doctor (God) will have the solution to meet all my needs. So, I find myself weighing all the pros and cons of this waiting period. I know the cons of not knowing if what you need will be available, no guarantee that things will be successful, or the losing of people who have been there from the start sometimes make the waiting period seem not worth it.

However, when you reflect on the pros of the waiting period, it is worthwhile. I have learned it is worth doing it scared because it allows God to be God and continue to work things out for my good. Since I am out of control in the Waiting Room, I have no other choice than to walk in faith. I believe the risk I am taking is worthwhile. I also have learned that the need for others' validations dies in the waiting period because it's not for others to understand. After all, it's not about you as a person, but God's purpose birthed through your life.

Although the Waiting Room period starts lonely, there is always a light at the end of the tunnel, and the 'doctor' sends his nurse to come out and call your name to come back and get serviced. Life is not happening to us but for us, and as we are experiencing life's challenges, it is not to disqualify us. It is to prepare us to fulfill the purpose God has placed us on this earth to fulfill. So when the opportunity shows up, one has already prepared for it during their Waiting Room period.

If you find yourself in a Waiting Room experience because life is starting to become overwhelming, find solstice in sharing your story. The women who are a part of this project have found power in sharing their voice and look to inspire you to do the same. The beauty of one's brain is constantly developing and creating new connections. We desire the stories in this anthology to create a new connection for you as you prepare for the doctor (God) to call you back to live out your life's purpose.

Mylira Green, LCSW of M. Green Enterprises, LLC.

Providing preventative services to lower the number of individuals in mental health facilities and people receiving post reactionary care.

Table of Contents

I

Breathing while HOLDING YOUR BREATH

DR. C. NICOLE HENDERSON, ED.D.

Dr. Nicole Henderson is an award-winning researcher, dynamic speaker, executive consultant, professor, and social entrepreneur who is passionate about helping the community thrive personally, academically, and professionally.

She is the founder and currently serves as the President and CEO of Collegiate Bridge, Inc., which empowers the next generation of students, to step confidently toward their future and achieve their college and career goals.

Dr. Henderson spent the bulk of her career creating college success pathways and training higher education administrators on developing college engagement and retention programming, while serving as the Dean of Student Affairs. She is now passionate about sharing her personal journey of surviving a toxic work environment to empower and guide women to walk into their full self by understanding and accepting the multi-dimensional nature of their being.

Dr. Henderson is a frequent conference and seminar speaker and trainer, typically speaking on issues of college equity, diversity, leadership, college readiness, student engagement, retention and accepting the multi-dimensional nature of you.

She holds a doctorate from Drexel University, a master's from the University of South Florida, and a bachelor's from the University of Florida.

In 2019 my life unraveled...

"Where is she?"' My husband yelled at the top of his lungs. I immediately bolted upstairs. I didn't even know who he was talking to or about, but I will never forget the fear and pain I heard in his voice that pierced me to my core. Something I never heard before. His voice shaking, he said my daughter's name and that they were doing CPR. My heart sank, and I immediately began holding my breath and praying. I knew something horrific happened.

My daughter, along with her new husband of only eight months and their four-month-old son were involved in a horrific car accident, which left my daughter in a coma with a traumatic brain injury. She was airlifted via medical helicopter to the trauma center undergoing immediate brain surgery removing half her skull to relieve the pressure on her brain to save her life. Her son was taken to the pediatric ICU at another hospital. My heart was shattered into a million broken pieces.

My husband grabbed his keys, I grabbed my purse, picked up our son, and we all jumped in the car and immediately began that two-hour trip (which seemed like ten) to the hospital. When I arrived at the hospital everything seemed surreal, but it did not stop me from running through and being overwhelmed by all these emotions of anger, sadness, confusion, and fear.

I found myself walking through ICU doors that would forever change my life. I walked into a room that resembled something out of an episode of Chicago Hope or House MD: monitors, tubes, machines beeping every few seconds, IVs dripping fluids into my child's veins, and a ventilator breathing for her. She was not awake yet! With every breath the machine took for her, my heart would break a little more.

Since her injuries were severe, the doctors prepared us for the worst. They said she may never wake from the coma and if she does, she may have suffered massive trauma to her brain ending her ability to regain normal function again. We were just waiting to see at this point. As I saw my beautiful daughter laying there fighting for her life, I gently held her hand, moved closer to her ear, and whispered how much I loved her and how proud I was of her. I reminded her of the amazing woman she was and told her to use the incredible fighting spirit she possessed to fight her way back to us, her new baby, and the amazing family she had just begun with her husband. Then my knees buckled. I did not realize that at that moment I stopped breathing. This is what happens when we go into shock or trauma: *We freeze and hold our breath.*

HOW DID I GET HERE?

I was completely numb. I was not numb because of my daughter's accident, although it was devastating to the depths of my soul. I was numb because I was already battered, bruised, and traumatized from spending the last four years fighting a daily battle of microaggressions and racelighting in a hostile work environment that simply did not value me as a woman of color. At that moment I was exhausted. I looked up, closed my eyes, and told God that I had no more to give. "Jesus, please take the wheel."

Looking back, I now realize that God prepared me for that very moment. But at that moment, I asked God how I got there. I spent years working to reach what I thought would be the pinnacle of my career. I earned my doctorate degree and became a college executive – a college dean, after three rounds of interviews, a full presentation, and eight hours of interviews across two campuses. Being a leader is not easy, especially when your workplace is hostile. I have experienced for years–the constant attempts to invalidate me by referring to all my white counterparts as "DR." but not me although we all have the exact same terminal degree. I was called a "quota hire" by my white counterparts to reject my qualifications for the position. I experienced the "secret meetings" held to discuss changes to the department I oversaw but somehow, I was mistakenly left off the meeting invite. In a direct attempt to undermine me, the "secret meeting" discussion became the agenda items on another larger college wide meeting, with questions and unnecessarily harsh feedback directed to me. It took a moment before I began to figure out what was taking place. As I questioned when this was all discussed, I was able to get the culprits to admit that I "mistakenly" was left off the meeting invite. They told me it was simply an oversight. So, we are to believe that a meeting took place to discuss my unit that I am responsible for providing oversight and no one in the meeting thought to question why I was not at the meeting? And at the second meeting, why were the questions directed at me when they knew I was not at the first meeting? Why was it not acknowledged that I was not at the meeting where this was discussed? When I asked these very questions, the response was that "I was being too sensitive and taking it out of context." This is textbook racelighting, a racial version of gaslighting.

It is hard to deal with a hostile work environment. Even if you have already found your voice and established yourself as a leader, it can be hard to feel strong when you are up against big issues like systematic racism. From day one of becoming a college dean, I found myself dealing with microaggressions and racism daily. The first couple years were hard, but as time went on and I became more outspoken against racism and discrimination, things got worse. I was the only Black female dean on the leadership team, until finally a second Black woman came on board. That did not stop the harassment or the racism though; I still found myself suffering from microaggressions regularly. Microaggressions, although subtle, are verbal or nonverbal racial insults that often fly under the radar. Oftentimes, a microaggression does not outright cross boundaries that would be considered discrimination based on legal protections, so it is difficult to prove. But over time they build up, become louder, bolder, and more aggressive creating a hostile work environment.

We have all heard the phrase "Don't quit your day job." It is easy to laugh it off, but when you are in a toxic work environment, you may find yourself on the edge of quitting your day job constantly. I would get anxious as I pulled into the parking lot each morning. I would pray in the car sometimes to tears. Asking God for strength to endure another day. I would recite Ephesians

6 as I walked to the building reminding myself to: *"put on the full armor of God, so that you can take your stand against the devil's schemes. Put on the full armor of God, so that when the day of evil comes, you may be able to stand your ground, and after you have done everything, to stand. Stand firm then, with the belt of truth buckled around your waist, with the breastplate of righteousness in place, and with your feet fitted with the readiness that comes from the gospel of peace. In addition to all this, take up the shield of faith, with which you can extinguish all the flaming arrows of the evil one. Take the helmet of salvation and the sword of the Spirit, which is the word of God."*

It was an everyday occurrence of subtle digs, email after email to human resources, or my supervisor making erroneous complaints and just some outright lies I had to defend. It created an unsafe and unhealthy environment and when I shared my concerns with the human resources department, I was told to "keep my eye on them." I had to document everything, every conversation in an attempt to protect myself because the deliberate attempts to undermine me were escalating. On several occasions, there were witnesses who agreed with me, in private, but who would not back me up or speak up because they feared retaliation, loss of promotion, or losing their job. Fear is the great silencer.

I spent more time and energy fighting lies, racists statements, microaggressions, and being marginalized than I did running my unit. It simply became exhausting. I filed a formal discrimination complaint hoping the college would begin a comprehensive investigation and address the systemic racism, they did not, and it was clear they did not care about my well-being and safety. I began to feel powerless. I felt paralyzed, and I realized that although I was breathing, I have been holding my breath the whole time.

While fighting the system, speaking up, and providing cover for others on my team, the unhealthy, unsafe, toxic work environment that I should have left years before, had me on the brink of mental and physical collapse. The work-related stress, toxicity within the system, bullying, and lack of support compromised my mental and physical health, nearly costing me my life. Microaggressions, although subtle, are powerful behaviors that cause extreme stress, anxiety, and trauma, especially for Black women in the workplace.

After suffering from chronic pain, chronic inflammation, chronic insomnia, being diagnosed with chronic depression and anxiety, steadily increasing medication, and three medical leaves, I made a conscious decision that I had to take control of my life. I came to the realization that this was not normal for a workplace and that there were other places where Black women are valued, could be happy and productive together—places where people actually cared about each other's well-being and success as much as their own. I deserved better and decided I would not settle for less.

I had to make a choice to resurrect that woman who went through life at 120 miles per hour, whose family said was always stuck on ready, the Doer

— that woman who was not going to let this break her. This is my life, and it was time to take control, rewrite my narrative, and reinvent myself.

IN THE WAITING ROOM

Despite not having a plan, any open doors, or opportunities in front of me, relying only on my faith and the support of my husband, after being on the job for 12 years, in the middle of a pandemic, I closed that door and bet on myself. I found myself in the hallway with no open doors on either side.

As a middle aged, well educated, highly accomplished, *seasoned* Black woman, I have learned a lot about life. One lesson: doors are a lie. When you are waiting for an open door, a closed door can feel like a heavy blow. A closed door is like a punch to the gut. It is like someone just told you that you are not good enough to be allowed in, surfacing all the old emotions of not *feeling good enough*. And then there are times when you reach out to push through a closed door and there is no handle on the other side! You are trapped! But are you?

What happens when you stop waiting for open doors? What happens when you realize that not all doors are open, that some of them will never be open? You can either stay locked up inside yourself forever or you can walk through whatever door is available at any given moment in time and make it yours. As a Black woman, I have spent my entire life fighting closed doors. This was no different.

As I prayed, I realized that is exactly what God was revealing to me. God had placed me in that space to learn and grow. God sees beyond closed doors, so we must learn to trust him when those doors close. Only God really knows what is best for us. After leaving that toxic environment behind, I had to figure out what steps I needed to take to reinvent myself, get healthy again, find my purpose and happiness once more! Then the excitement of the journey to better was greater than the initial fear I experienced by closing the door. I began to see the blessing of being in this space.

"It's not what happens to you, it's how you react to it that matters." I used this Epictetus quote to set me on the path of growth. I began a spiritual journey of letting go of who I used to be to become the woman I was meant to be. I began to let go of my old identity of who I thought I needed to be often based on what I thought I needed to be. The problem lies in our attachment to the story we build. We all live our lives like we are the protagonist in a story, making choices and navigating relationships based on what we believe will ultimately serve the greater purpose of getting us where we want to go. The problem is that life does not actually work like that; this is not fiction. We become so absorbed in the details that we fail to make the most of this one life we have to live, and we tend to over-identify with the roles we play. So, I let go of Dr. Nicole Henderson and just became Nicole again.

HOW TO REGAIN CONTROL

We can take control of our own destinies by reinventing ourselves and finding purpose in novel places. The first step to reinventing yourself while in the waiting room is to start by taking care of yourself. It can be hard to do this when you are still reeling from the trauma of having worked in such an environment, but it is important to remember that you are worth taking care of. You deserve to be happy. Make sure that you are taking time for yourself. If possible, spend some time alone with no distractions. This can be difficult if you have children or other obligations that require your attention—but it is essential that you find a way to carve out this time for yourself. This may mean getting up early before anyone else wakes up or staying up late when everyone else has gone to sleep.

The first step towards being happy is to build your faith-walk and reconnect with God. I began by getting up before everyone else so that I could have quiet time with just me and God. I started a daily gratitude journal so that I could once again start off seeing the good in my life. Although I had so many journals I started, I decided to begin this journey with a brand new journal for the brand-new Middle-Aged Goddess I was becoming! I bought a cute pink one that inspired joy and positive energy just by looking at it. I still have my pink journal that I used during my journey. It helped me approach each morning with a positive frame of mind and gave me comfort knowing that I have a fantastic foundation to build upon every day — no matter what may happen. In my quiet space, I began each day from a place of gratitude by writing just *one* thing for which I was grateful. I kept it simple. Simplicity is the key. I then read my short, morning devotional and then would write what my heart was saying and what my heart was hearing. Again, I kept it simple. Sometimes, I just wrote one word and sometimes a paragraph flowed. The key is to be silent and hear what your heart is saying.

Gospel music was also a crucial part of regaining my control. Music has a way of hitting our soul and sometimes putting into words what we are feeling but could not find the words to express. During this time, the one song that I played daily that carried me through my darkest moments was *You Know My Name* by Tasha Cobbs Leonard. The lyrics spoke to the depths of my soul in a time when I needed to know God knew my name.

He knows my name

Yes, he knows my name

He knows my name

Yes, he knows my name

And oh, how he walks with me

Yes oh, how he talks with me

And oh how he tells me

That I am his own

You know my name

You know my name

And oh how you comfort me

And oh how you counsel me

Yet it still amazes me

That I am your friend

So now

I pour out

My heart to you

Here in

Your presence

I am made new

So now

I pour out

My heart to you

Here in

Your presence

I am made new

You know my name

Said you know my name (you know my name)

And oh how you walk with me

Oh how you talk with me (you talk with me)

Oh how you tell me

I am your own

Oh you got to know me

So I trust you with my life, yeah

No, no fire can burn me

No battle can turn me

No mountain can stop me

Cause you hold my hand

And now I'm walking in your victory

Cause your power is within me

No giant can defeat me

Cause you hold my hand

No fire can burn me

No battle can turn me

No mountain can stop me

All because (you hold my hand)

Oh and I'm walking, yeah, in your victory

Cause your power, it lives within me

No giant can defeat me

You hold my hand

I said no fire can burn me

No battle, it's already won

No mountain can stop me (not gonna stop me)

Cause you hold my hand ('cause you hold my hand)

Now I'm walking in your victory

Cause your power it lives within me

No giant can defeat me

You hold my hand ('cause you hold my hand)

You hold my hand (you hold my hand)

To be afraid, no (you hold my hand)

I don't have to be afraid, no (you hold my hand)

I don't have to be afraid (you hold my hand)

You hold my hand (you hold my hand)

You hold my hand (you hold my hand)

I'm so in love with you (you hold my hand)

I'm so in love with you (you hold my hand)

You hold my hand (you hold my hand)

Oh (you hold my hand)

You hold my hand (you hold my hand)

You babe (you hold my hand)

You know my name

You know my name,

You know my name

You know my name

Oh how you walk with me

Oh how you walk with me

I'm in love with you, Lord

Oh how you talk with me

Just to commune with you

Oh how you tell me I belong to you

That I am your own

Because I had gotten to such a low point both physically and mentally, I focused on getting both physically and mentally fit. Coming from a state of chronic stress and depression, it's like operating in what I call a purple funk. You are not firing on all cylinders. So, before you can begin to think about what's next or make any life decisions you must be healthy both physically and mentally.

Give yourself permission to feel the way you do. Get a therapist who can help you process your feelings. Believe me, there will be a lot of feelings and emotions and trauma to process. If you're feeling angry, sad, or any other negative emotion, it's okay. You have every right to experience those feelings, and your emotional state is as valid as anyone else's. I had so many emotions I had to work through and process. Our bodies hold on to trauma. It takes work to fully process it. Just because we are able to push it down, which I can do really well, does not mean that it is gone. It is ok to seek out professional help to get your mental health in check. Just think of it like going to the gym for your emotional and mental wellbeing, just like you go to the gym for your physical wellbeing.

It is also important for you to reconnect with old friends who fully support you and bring positivity, laughter, and joy into your life. Surrounding yourself with positive people will help you become more positive and begin to see life from a positive perspective. For the same reason, do not hang around negative people. Negative energy breeds negative energy. Positive energy only.

Get up and move physically. It does not have to be the gym. I hired a trainer who came to my house because I was not ready for the gym. The pain in my body was too severe. I also began walking. I started with just one mile and worked my way up to five miles. Just get active and move. And I cannot say this enough practice self-care! We have heard this over and over, but when we are in this space of waiting, self-care is part of the growth. Self-care is an important part of being able to take care of others when they need us most—so if we do not take care of ourselves first physically, emotionally, and mentally, how can we be there for others? Self-care is more than manicures and pedicures! Make sure that every day includes actions that bring joy into your life: go out with friends and family; watch a movie; read a book; meditate; go for a walk; listen to music; go dancing. Whatever makes you happy! That is self-care!

As I began to grow physically, mentally, and emotionally, I regained clarity. I ended all medication, and all my medical reports were once again normal. My physician was ecstatic about my progress and all my reports. She shared that it is clear now that we were really treating an environment because everything is back to normal. I was floored, but happy. I felt like I did my work, and I was fully back even though I was still in the waiting room.

I was fully out of the purple funk and could begin to reflect on what is really important in life for me in this next stage. I was excited at the possibilities, and I was not interested in what society says or by what is on social media, but only what really makes me thrive and not merely survive. I was ready to make a plan for myself and figure out what kind of life makes me happy, what kind of job would make me happy then I'm going after it! I felt like James Brown, "I'm Back!

As I began asking myself what I want out of life, the opportunities and the doors began to appear and open. I realized that I love the work I do, just not in the environment. The greatest realization was that I never had the opportunity to really be Dr. Nicole Henderson because I never fully walked into Dr. Nicole Henderson on my own terms. As I reflected, I realized that I never celebrated passing my dissertation defense and becoming Dr. Henderson. In fact, I defended alone with no family, friends, or support, and then I returned to work, out of fear, and worked the rest of the day as if nothing happened. How sad was that.

But that is why God had me in the waiting room. I had to get to this place of freedom and clarity, which led me back to Dr. C. Nicole Henderson and starting my consulting company, Dr. C. Nicole Henderson consulting. I was in my happy place and enjoying every moment. It was a lot of work, but it was work I loved! I was blown away by the success of my consulting firm. I was unable to serve all the families and organizations that contacted me, so I partnered with other colleagues to fully serve the community. I was truly in a season of overflow! I went on and founded Collegiate Bridge, a non-profit committed to increasing the higher education attainment and leadership pipeline for Black students by providing the college knowledge, skills, and network needed to get them to college graduation. Collegiate Bridge is phenomenally successful, and I have amassed the highest level of praise and testimonials for the work we are doing. It is only by the grace of God and this journey through the waiting room that I can say I have fully emerged stronger, wiser, happier, and ready to walk in my full purpose as Dr. C. Nicole Henderson. I plan to continue to work to empower the next generation of Black leaders by empowering Black college students and Black women with the knowledge on how to successfully navigate the workplace and avoid the pitfalls that I encountered.

WHAT I LEARNED

On my healing journey to a happy, thriving, woman fully living on purpose, I have learned some valuable lessons I want to share.

1. You are in control of your life– You have the ability and right to create the life you want.

2. It is okay to be happy and content in your own skin. This society has a way of making Black women feel as if we must prove we belong. We do not have to. We are enough simply because we are.

3. Never let anyone, or anything stop you from living your life to the fullest. When you find yourself in any environment that does not serve you, leave. **Do not** remain and endure the pain and trauma. It will negatively impact your health and heart.

4. Take responsibility for your own happiness and make yourself happy before you can make others happy. You must take some time to do things that make you feel happy. Whatever makes you happy make it part of your daily routine, not your weekly routine.

5. Approach each morning with a positive frame of mind that gives you a foundation to build upon every day — no matter what may happen. The most successful optimists never forget what they have to be thankful for. It is important to feel grateful for what we have in the present and for me it was my incredible faith, my extremely supportive and loving family, and friends, and most importantly, an optimistic attitude.

You may walk through nights so dark that they seem like they will never end. You may even forget what it even means to feel joy. But I am here to tell you that the dawn will come, and you will sing again. There is hope. The promise is that the Lord your God is with you. That is the reason to keep your heart awake just a little bit longer. I know because when the doctors had no hope for us; when the doctors said my daughter may not wake again,

I did not believe them. I stood on faith and knew that God would provide. My daughter did emerge from her coma and began her battle to fully recover. While she has not fully recovered, and I do not know that she ever will, what I do know is that she taught me that we are more than conquerors and we can never lose with God on our side. God does not want us broken in any area of our life. He wants us whole. I continue to pursue the wholeness in my life every day. I pray that you too will pursue the wholeness in you!

Five Tips while in The Waiting Room

1. Don't rush through the transition. When we are moving from one point to another, and when we find ourselves in between, we tend to crave the transition. In reality, it's a technique of distraction, an easy way to relieve the pressure of feeling stuck. Spend time in the transition to grow and learn.

2. Get anchored in your faith. Create quiet time with God each day. It's quality over quantity. Ten quality moments with God are better than 45 minutes with your mind wandering to your To Do list. Remember to pray a short prayer and then be silent and listen for God's voice. Listen to your heart, because God will speak to your heart.

3. Give yourself permission to relax, soften, and grow. Being our best selves doesn't mean being perfect 24/7. Give yourself permission to relax, celebrate your daily victories big and small and resist any self-criticism if things don't go as planned, because they usually won't.

4. Practice daily affirmations. Get a daily affirmations app on your phone and set it up to send you affirmations at least three times a day. I recommend the "I am" app. That is the one I use, and I have five affirmations sent throughout the day. They are like mini power boosters for your soul.

5. Find a really great therapist to help you process and work through all the emotions you will experience from being in a place of uncertainty. Before you can begin to think about what's next or make any life decisions you must be healthy, both emotionally and mentally.

Acknowledgements

There were so many people who helped me get to this point in my life. First and foremost, all praises to God who is the head of my life.

A very special thank you to my incredible husband, David, who has been my rock for nearly 40 years! I thank you for your love, your calming spirit, and for anchoring our family.

To my son Miles, thank you for your insight, support, and working to leave this world better than how you found it. To my daughter Kristian, thank you for being my personal cheerleader. To my son-in-law Jason, thank you for all the wonderful gourmet meals. To both of you, thank you for the pure joy of my grandsons.

To my siblings, thank you for your continuous love, support, and just being there for me. A very special thank you to my girlfriends and former colleagues who truly provided an amazing amount of support and encouragement during some of the darkest moments.

Finally, although she is no longer with me on this earth, I must thank my mother, Johnnie M. Parris, who was always my number one advocate and the wind beneath my wings. My mom was a pioneer, trailblazer, and civil rights activist who had an unrelenting pursuit of an equitable society. She taught me the importance of faith, family, and standing up for the Black community. I stand on her shoulders, and I am who I am because of her.

Dedication

"Beautiful is the woman who inspires herself to believe she has the power to accomplish anything and everything."

This chapter is dedicated to all the beautiful Black women seeking balance in their lives. This chapter is an expression of my hope. I hope it will inspire you to take the first step toward real self-empowerment. My prayer is that you will begin to walk your own path, then gradually run with confidence, and finally soar into your power to achieve your purpose.

Reflections

_____
_____
_____
_____
_____
_____
_____
_____
_____
_____
_____
_____
_____
_____
_____
_____
_____
_____
_____
_____

Reflections

_____

_____

_____

_____

_____

_____

_____

_____

_____

_____

_____

_____

_____

_____

_____

_____

_____

_____

_____

_____

Reflections

CHAPTER

11

W.A.I.T:
Why am I so Troubled?

DR. SHANA WILLIAMS

Dr. Shana Monique Williams is a Charleston, South Carolina native. Dr. Williams loves being a nurse and doctoral prepared Psychiatric Nurse Practitioner. She is passionate about the care and engagement of those experiencing behavioral health illnesses, and is a part of a collaborative team who impacts the future of the nursing profession. Shana currently lives in Sumter, South Carolina with her nine year old son Christopher John . She also has a 22 year old son Shane, who is currently in the United States Navy. She is extremely proud of her daughter-in love Tazhane and grandson Kaison Amir. Kaison is the cutest grandson and she wants to give him the world. She also loves her bonus four; Cedney, Justice, AnnMarie and Amir.

Dr. Williams enjoys spending time with the love of her life, Mike, her family, fellowshipping with friends, and sorors in the Gamma Xi Omega chapter of Alpha Kappa Alpha Sorority Inc! She also enjoys reading, watching movies,walks in the park, and what she likes to call her sanctuary, which is the beach!

Shana lives her life by a certain philosophy: I love people and I desire to make sure that everyone I encounter has the best life and lives it unapologetically.

"I don't mind waiting"

by Juanita Bynum is one of my favorite songs. I listen to it often while riding to work, throughout the day and when feeling stressed/overwhelmed. No matter the version I listen to, I always find myself singing it at the top of my lungs. It has been a refuge for me, especially during the toughest times of my life. The lyrics are symbolic and the message is clear.

You know, sometimes in life, situations are going to occur where you may look to the left or the right and you can't find any answers and you can't find anybody to help you, but I'm reminded of the Word that says they that wait upon the Lord, He shall renew their strength. They shall mount up on wings as eagles. They shall run and not be weary. They shall walk and not faint. Come on. You've got to learn how to wait.

I don't mind waiting.
I don't mind waiting.
I don't mind waiting, on You Lord.
I don't mind waiting.
I don't mind waiting.
I don't mind waiting, on You Lord.

I remember praying these words: "God I don't mind waiting for you to provide me with what I need/want. I will wait on you Lord to bless me." Yet, while I waited, my immediate thought was that if I didn't mind waiting on the Lord, why was I still so troubled.

As a child, we were taught to wait no matter how impatient we were with our parents because important things require time. Eventually we learn to wait and learn that things will happen over time. We learn that being impatient changes nothing. We learn that God has his timing and that while he has a process so does everything in our lives. So waiting is a process–a process with no explanation. Everyone can relate to the process of how certain things work. When you have an appointment at a specific place and time, you are required to check-in once you get there. You verify your information, fill out paperwork, and may even make a payment. Once check-in is completed, most of the time you still must wait even though you may have arrived early, but especially if you are late. The wait begins as you enter the W.A.I.Ting room and take a seat.

As you endure the process of waiting, the Waiting Room can often be crowded or empty; loud or silent; messy or neat; cold or warm. The Waiting Room can also be full of distractions such as watching TV or talking to people around you. . Yet the Waiting Room can also bring your day and your life into focus. The Waiting Room can be a place you think or a place you worry. The Waiting Room can be a place where you can stand alone or sit next to someone you do not know. The Waiting Room can be a place of faith but also a place of doubt. The Waiting Room can also be the main place where you feel completely safe or where the feeling of trouble begins. However, eventually your time will come for you to be directed out of the Waiting Room and into a hallway.

The hallway is another area where you continue to walk down with many doors. Some of the doors are closed, cracked, or open. Some open doors may need to be pushed open and some closed doors may need to be locked. Sometimes you will have to stand in the hallway to have more information collected or have other information clarified. Sometimes the business in the hallway makes you wish you could go back to the Waiting Room until you are ready to enter the hallway when it is not as hard to stand in. The doors can be even worse with unresolved emotions, past traumas and any and everything in between. The doors can even be things that you have not even bothered to think about. Let me tell you about my journey in the W.A.I.T.ing room.

Who is Shana Monique I always wondered? I spent many years, approximately about twenty, quietly sitting in my Waiting Room. Not sure if I truly ever entered the hallway fully to even explore the doors. I looked at some of the opened doors but lacked the confidence to walk up or even enter. Some doors were off limits due to my fear. While other doors were partially open due to lying to myself; I prayed to have other doors closed and the occupants to leave so that the room could be cleaned.

Some will say twenty years is a long time to figure out who you are, but I spent twenty years thinking, processing, and wondering who I had become.

Twenty years of trying to fit in. Twenty years of trying to understand. Twenty years of sitting or lying on a couch talking through the hardships of my life. Twenty years of feeling misunderstood or appearing cold. Twenty years of adjusting to whatever surrounding I was in.

I grew up with two parents, one brother I never knew, and one sister. I technically was the middle child, but I was also a rainbow baby (the baby after a miscarriage, a symbol of renewal and hope). My tribe was made up of thirteen aunts, thirty-nine first cousins, two blood uncles, and five best friends. I grew up feeling left-out most of the time. For most of the twenty years I worried about what others thought of me. Not because I sought to impress them but for most of my early years, I did not get a chance to know others. I was the shy new kid who was very smart but moved a lot–five times from the age of five to ten years old.

We moved from Charleston to Beaufort, South Carolina where I started at the local elementary school and attended the after school daycare. Then, during recess in the second grade, I was suddenly taken out of school and we packed up and moved to St. Petersburg Florida. I remember hating riding in the car, and that trip was the longest trip ever. I remember getting into my first fight my second day at the school and made one friend that lived in the same apartment complex. We attended the black church that was packed every Sunday and I started to sing in the children's choir. However, that was short-lived as we then moved back to Beaufort South Carolina where I saw the older version of friends only to then move to Sumter, South Carolina. Sumter became my home in the fifth grade and although we would often return to the roots of Charleston South Carolina. Every holiday, during the summer, weekends became more frequent as now in Sumter we were closer to our family. Both of my parents originated from the area and so it was not hard to see all of the family in one weekend. Yet even surrounded by all this family I was troubled. Just typing this makes me feel like I was that 10 yo all over again seeking acceptance, feeling lost and wanting to find my place in the world. As I sat in my Waiting Room, I wanted to find my happiness. I wanted my family to embrace me. I wanted to be inspired. The catch was, I was ready to enter the hallway to pursue the happiness I thought was real.

Happiness did not come as easy as I envisioned in my teenage years. The weekend and holiday trips to Charleston were constant. Yet I started to create the friendships I wanted to have and felt like I did not fit with my cousins in the den, I was too old for my other cousins, and I could not be in the room with the adults. I shut this door and moved on to another door and decided to go to another door in the hallway as I was ready to be embraced by someone in my family besides my mother.

Well, I did not get to play victim and I did not feel like a victim as I got to know some of my family on a level that others did not. My maternal grandmother and I talked often about how her life was growing up and how she wanted something different for her children and grandchildren. She often challenged me to stop being "so soft" and show every cousin how valuable I was. She talked to me about how I could begin to make friends and how they could become like my family. She also taught me how to open myself and trust that I could make the right friends, and those who cared for me would not walk away from me. We often would sneak off to Hampton Park as she used to walk to the bus stop and often I would wonder if she was walking all the way to work, which I knew was blocks away. She taught me that sometimes being alone was necessary and practicing patience and victory can sustain you in your toughest times. She was the realest woman I knew that stood her ground until the day she died. She taught me that you did not need degrees, material things, or money to make your life what you wanted it to be. I always saw her as the "hardcore grandmother" who didn't' take no junk off no one and made sure she and she alone would make sure her children had what they needed no matter what. She was not going to allow me to feel lost and never let me feel sorry for myself. "You are a victim if you choose to be!" I used to feel like she was harsh, but I know she cared. She embraced me in my Waiting Room, she pushed my fears and even helped me kick down some doors. Although she is no longer with me, she made a baddie!

My paternal grandmother inspired me with the way she cared for her husband and children with her gentle spirit and soft-spoken voice. She inspired me with her heart. She was real like my other grandmother but had a way of softening the blow. However, if you pushed her too far, she let you know you were crossing a boundary. She inspired me with the way she dealt with people while in her Waiting Room grieving her life and now that she is standing in her hallway, she continues to inspire me to remain intentional in having a big heart and sharing it with those that don't misunderstand it. Her Alzheimer's disease had caused her to not remember much about me yet she inspires me with understanding that as you start to walk down your hallway some steps you may not remember, some doors may close in your face but at some other season in your life some doors look familiar and can be open in another phase in your life. Even if you must face that phase of your life alone to change the narrative.

ALONE IN MY CALLING

I was never good at being alone and in fact I hated it. I still do to this very moment however I found that this was the best phase of my life. Being alone was the time I got to know Shana Monique, I got to know what I liked. Being alone helped me understand that the blasted Waiting Room was where you could meet new people and experience life on a new level. Some of the encounters in the Waiting Room have changed my life on so many levels, it taught me to be true to myself and accept myself. Changing the narrative was a part of my journey, and yet I was becoming a functional troubled person. This was the hardest part of being in the hallway and once again I wished to go back to the Waiting Room where I did not have to feel any emotions. In the Waiting Room I could hide, but there have been times when my Waiting Room was empty. It was empty emotionally and although my grandmothers, my parents, and my sisters were sitting in the room with me my narrative was not victory.

I was now in my senior year of high school, and I still had not changed the narrative. I was out of the Waiting Room because I ran from someone I knew and trusted who was in my Waiting Room. Someone who I valued as a friend became a door on the hallway that was off limits as it threatened the feeling of being embraced, the feeling of being inspired, he had changed the narrative and I was standing in my hallway afraid, and I felt abandoned by God. I felt that same feeling of not fitting in and not being understood. My sadness was misinterpreted by some family members as me feeling that I was too good for them. This resulted in me only allowing two women in my heart: my Aunt Christine and Aunt Marilyn. Aunt Christine and Marilyn are who I happened to be the closest to as they helped me re-open a door and kept a very hard secret for me. They protected me and understood me on so many levels.

Aunt Christine affectionately known as "Chrissy" understood my calling to help others at their time of need and introduced me to nursing. I would get exposed to nursing in a way that would not only create another door but lead me down a career path that would be life changing.

My first encounter with a nurse first came when I had my oldest son, Shane Michael, and Nurse Jean was so kind to me. She talked to me after I was placed in the postpartum unit. Although Nurse Jean knew I was going to give up my son for adoption, she went against "what everyone thought was best," she allowed me to hold my baby for most of the night and encouraged me to talk to him. She also took pictures of him and reminded me of how "life comes full circle", and I would see him again, but I had to be ready. I knew she had other patients that night, but Jean made me feel like a mom, she gave me a time and space to cry, and love on my baby that I thought I would never see again. Jean even stayed to assist me to sign the adoption papers. She gave me the pictures of Shane and told me to never close the door to meeting him at the age of 18 (when he could seek me out).

Aunt Christine made sure my attraction to the nursing profession remained in my hallway yet somehow, she and I still ended up in the Waiting Room. Again, Aunt Christine sat with me in the Waiting Room as once again I was troubled. However, she was patient until I was ready to walk through the door of being a minority in the nursing profession. She taught me about how to be the kind of nurse that cares, the kind of nurse that will be the "exception to the rule." She continues to guide me to this day!! She also continues to inspire me daily with her strength to "stand tall and proud in breaking generational patterns" and continuing to keep the same momentum Marilyn established during my time with her in the Waiting Room.

Aunt Marilyn sat with me and Christine in the Waiting Room to help me get back to myself when I sat out the Fall of 1998 from my first year of college to grieve giving up my son for adoption. For three months, I sat in my room and journaled. Aunt Marilyn challenged me to keep the door of my mind and heart open, yet I did not want to leave the Waiting Room. She pushed me out of the Waiting Room and lit the path on the dark hallway. She challenged me to light the hallway and start to work on maintaining my- self-love, womanhood, and to be a butterfly that continuously evolves and adjusts to my surroundings. "You do not get to be a victim, you push and push until you get to your dreams, peace and happiness." She would always say that no matter how I felt. She would not let me feel sorry for myself but would always encourage me to process. She stood with me in my hallway when I graduated with my bachelors, masters and we talked about me going for my doctorate. She would not let me become a victim or lose my self-esteem until her death in 2009. Although she is no longer physically standing in the hallway with me, she is in my heart. We spent her last days talking about how I must remember who I am, stay on my grind, and keep my mind and heart open to how life will change my plans. She told me to keep the door open even when I was misunderstood or when others do not see the real me. Although I did not think it was her last day, she made sure someone was going to be there to help her butterfly, as she affectionately called me, to embrace life.

Aunt Jane, the fourth oldest of my mom's sisters, became the person that showed me how to embrace the beauty of life. She made sure I understood how to be a woman with a plan B (nope not the pill). We would sit at Hampton Park for hours on one particular bench to talk about life. She also helped me understand that every experience shapes how we live. She made me look at life as a woman that made her life possible no matter what. Guess what she did? She put me back in the Waiting Room to "slow down and embrace the present but also prepare for my future." We sat in that Waiting Room until I understood "life has a way of testing your faith and you have to know it's an inside job." As we sat in the Waiting Room, I screamed "What am I missing?" She told me I had to understand; and I spent a lot of time in the Waiting Room focusing on that statement. She would always say that God will sustain you! Little did I know how that statement would lead me back into the hallway to open and go through the door of divorce and single parenthood. Man, did I need a Plan B to prepare for this. Does the emotional, spiritual, and physical trouble ever end?

Aunt Delores and Carolyn were my paternal aunts that unknowingly sat in my Waiting Room with me to teach me about heartbreak and the love from your family. They did not realize everyone sitting in my Waiting Room had a purpose. "You can still move forward when life hits you hard." You can have the best life and start a new chapter unapologetically." I watched them from afar during my single life, my marriage and my divorce. They had the most impact on my decision to choose myself after 20 years. "Nothing is wrong with starting over, you can always change how your chapter begins and ends." "Be your own narrator and your family will stand with you." They taught me about forgiveness and love. They taught me to not hate the person but to dislike their actions. I valued this in them and even though they did not know about Shane Michael until much later, they would never know how much I watched and learned from their wisdom.

While my aunts and uncles who knew I was troubled were in the Waiting Room and hallway, my parents understood my troubles and took all their life lessons and applied it to my childhood, teenage years, and adulthood. My parents taught me about seeing the big picture no matter how troubled I was. Even when they did not understand my emotion or my broken spirit and heart, they made me understand how important the Waiting Room was. The Waiting Room may have provided distraction at times but that was where you focus, evaluate life and fall in love with me first. Yes, you can check in at the registration desk and others will join you in the Waiting Room until your time comes, which can be troubling. But your hallway is another level to you getting to know yourself and others getting to know you. The hallway represented life experiences and it held my future. Whoever was in the Waiting Room, they could not get access to my hallway unless I let them scan into the hallway. This is what I needed to be careful about. Often, I could not understand how that hallway was so full of themes and emotions and what doors to open, what doors to peek around and what doors to leave closed. The Waiting Room and the hallway can also bring positive people, places, and things into your life, but you must ask yourself the following first:

1. Why am I so troubled?
2. Is being troubled mean that I cannot function?
3. How can I become a baddie?
4. How do I prepare for the full circle of life?
5. Why do I keep going to the Waiting Room?
6. What can I do to embrace the experience of the Waiting Room?
7. What can I do about the hallway?
8. Who should be in the Waiting Room?
9. Do I know who I am in the Waiting Room?
10. Do I know who I am in the hallway??
11. Is faith really an inside job?
12. How do I not become a victim?
13. How do I push forward?
14. How do I choose myself?
15. How can I focus on the present?
16. Is the hallway dark or is God changing the scene?

17. Will God sustain me in the Waiting Room?

18. How will God sustain me in my hallway?

19. What will happen if no one sees me?

20. How do I change the narrative?

Twenty questions over 20 years and I finally was able to arrive at a time where I was not troubled. 20 years of feeling disappointed, alone despite being surrounded by so many influential people. Did I have a rough childhood? No, my parents made sure I felt love, understood how family can be healthy but also supported each other through tough times. Yet over the course of 20 years, and various seasons; my spirit, physical being and love of myself was restored. Lord, it takes some time, but I learned that you can be troubled in waiting for things to be better.. You can be a baddie and keep going to the Waiting Room and being patient in your season which is only temporary but, you can embrace the experience of the Waiting Room and push forward, work on your inside and your faith. You cannot be a victim and allow others to assist you in choosing yourself, this requires you to be your own light in that dark hallway to see how God will sustain you when no one sees you. When I change the narrative, I can go back to the Waiting Room and wait patiently for someone to see me, to understand who I am and how I can evolve as a butterfly to walk along my hallway and go through any door.

Now 30 years later, I am in the hallway with a love from my childhood. Mike D found me in a very happy yet lonely doorway seeking love. He encouraged me to come through the door that I kept peeking around the entrance. He has shown me how one man can see and value everything, even the imperfect flaws, and still love me. He is watching me grow and has become my number one fan. Life has begun and it is effortless to love. I did not think I would love again; I did not think I would even open my heart to trust someone again. However, this time I am whole within myself first. I am my best friend, and he adds to that! We have laughed together and cried together, and for once I have left the Waiting Room.

My heart and mind is open–open to the full circle of life to find me and to love me as much as I love myself. And guess what, I am not troubled!

Five Tips while in The Waiting Room

1. Grieve the old you, who you were before. Walk through the emotions of figuring out who you are, what you like, why you feel how you feel, where you want to be, and how to be happy.

2. Journal about your journey– the good, the bad, the hard times, the happy times. Get out of your head and put It to paper. Set your boundaries about your journey. Read about it as you grow and embrace your greatness.

3. Find your place of peace! Where is the one place you can be alone, be vulnerable, be free, and not engage in drama? There is nothing wrong with disconnecting. Be selfish as peace is priceless.

4. Cry, Cry, and cry some more. Release the frustration you feel, release the stress you feel, and let the tears flow as they may.

5. Listen to those who value you. Sit in silence and become aware of what you feel. There is nothing wrong with being quiet and moving in silence when your light is dim and reconnection is needed. You must be prepared for when it's time to get up and walk into the Hallway.

Acknowledgments

To my parents, Tyrone and Kathleen.... Thank you for being the parents that God said this woman is your assignment and you build her up to accomplish any and everything she puts her mind to. She is your gem that will shine.

To my one and only sister, Shari....we have been rocking hard since 1985 and nothing will ever change the love I have for the one woman who has seen me and pushed me to be the best sister ever!! Let's brick them!

To my aunts, uncles, and cousins... Love will always be true, life will always be real and no matter what troubles we face... we are family and I love y'all.

To my brothers John and Tony... You know how we do!! Embrace your differences, iron sharpens iron and drop that wisdom for dat spirit! LOL!

To Kim, Vicky and Vonne... thanks for reminding me that life can change in a second and life is what you want it to be. Thank you for your love, support and encouragement when starting over was hard, when light was dim, and reconnection was needed.

To my best friends Sean and Isaiah… Thank you for all your "old man" and "Superman" wisdom and for reminding me to never stop going after all I deserve. You both have always been there when being myself was hard and tiring.

To Dawn, Jennifer, Teshia and Veronica… When healing was real, and the trash needed to be taken out, y'all helped me dump it, drop all the bags, and stand in my truth.

Kim and Carlton… My silent life investors. Thank you for your encouraging messages and love when I felt alone, forgetting about my awesomeness and reminders to "keep going."

Debbie, you are an amazing woman, and I cannot thank God enough for placing you in my life. God has laid a path to greatness through you and I am ready to walk it. I look forward to more!!

To my heartbeats… I hope my healing through this chapter reminds you that life can be rough but you have the foundation to keep building all you desire. I love each of you for what you individually add to me in my blessing to be a mom!! I love all of my seven angels which make my life complete.

Mike D… You have helped me be me again and remind me that you can change the channel, turn the page, and begin a new chapter. Now I believe in the truest of love, peace, and effortless happiness. I love you forever. Thank you for finding me and starting me back at one! #lifeisjustbeginning

Dedication

To the women and men who are waiting to be seen, heard and validated…. here it is.. You see yourself; you hear yourself and everyday remind yourself of your worth and you are happy where you are!!! Be unapologetic, give grace and forgive yourself!! Do not settle and love yourself!!

Reflections

_____

_____

_____

_____

_____

_____

_____

_____

_____

_____

_____

_____

_____

_____

_____

_____

_____

_____

_____

_____

_____

_____

Reflections

_____

_____

_____

_____

_____

_____

_____

_____

_____

_____

_____

_____

_____

_____

_____

_____

_____

_____

_____

III

Girl, get up
MY TALITHA KUOM
EXPERIENCE

LATONYA D. BLUE

LaTonya D. Blue was born and raised in Lancaster Virginia, a small town known as the Northern Neck area, born to Lawrence Palmer and Diana Brown. She was raised by both her maternal and paternal Grandmothers: Florence Baptist and Eliza Rice. LaTonya is the wife of Clifton Blue, mother of two kids:Kionté and T'Kāla Brown, and grandmother of two: Ja'Kye and Ayahna Brown.

LaTonya has been working in the nursing field as a caregiver for over 25 years. Through her upbringing, she learned a lot of values, morals, principles, and most of all how to treat people with respect. She takes pride in her nursing career and working with all types of people.

In 2019, LaTonya became an entrepreneur, as led by God, and started a cleaning and care service: Purposely Cleaning & Care Services, LLC. Also in 2019, God instructed LaTonya to start an on-line ministry named Girl, Give Me Your Hand Ministry & Women's Empowerment Group. She has helped heal several dozens of women and helped them find their purpose. She's an avid writer and follower of Christ. She plans to one day travel the world helping to heal the people of God.

In April 2022, she became a Co-Owner of her second business: Higher Peak Coaching/Counseling & Outreach Ministries, LLC. LaTonya will put her Life Coach, Spiritual Coaching certification, Introductory Child Counseling and Addiction Counseling Certification to use along with other degrees she will soon get.

She enjoys family time and when she is not working or doing ministry, she's planning a nice family day or weekend to love on her family.

What better time to start writing my story than now?

It seems that almost directly after the very moment that I gave God my "yes" to being a part of this anthology, all hell began to break loose in my family. Some of the worst things beyond my imagination have happened. The enemy really wanted me to throw in the towel on this, *but* he's a liar! Because I serve a God who is bigger than any circumstance or situation and the same God who has delivered, healed, broken chains and set me free shall be there for my family also. So here I am, pushing my way forth. I served the devil notice and demanded, "You will not take me back to places that God has already delivered me from!" This includes the spirit of procrastination. Here is my story on how God revived me from my "Dead Season" while in the Waiting Room.

Hailing from a small town in Virginia, you would think that who I'd become was from my upbringing. God had to allow me to go through and grow through some trials and tribulations. I had to be able to see his glory in every experience I'd gone through. He needed to get my attention because up until 2019, I was merely existing. Life was on autopilot, and I watched as my days passed by. Almost like looking through the lens of a third person. I was not living at all; just simply going through the motions. There was a constant gaping and numbness in my life. My life looks different now that I have nearly reformed faith. I walk with the Lord on a daily basis. I'm excited because I now know what it means to live. Just as God restored the world from nothing as He did in Genesis, He did for me. God gave me a new beginning.

In the winter of 2019, I experienced the worst heartbreak of my life. I was so devastated that the man I had given so many years of my life to, had turned his back on me. How could he? Is all that I could think of. I couldn't eat, sleep or even breathe. I was beginning to suffocate on my thoughts. It consumed me. Depression slowly began creeping in. God was tugging on my heart. What I now realize is that God no longer wanted me to die of the flesh. He was breaking me into position. He wanted to make my name great. He wanted to promote me. The Bible says "The Lord is close to the brokenhearted and saves those who are crushed in spirit" (Psalm 34:18, NIV)." God was tugging on my heart; what I realize now is that He was calling me to die of my flesh and surrender all unto Him. I had to be destroyed in order for him to rebuild and place me into the position for which He desired for me. God yearned to use me as a vessel for His good. I could no longer be disobedient and deny the calling over my life. The Bible says, "The Lord is close to the brokenhearted and saves those who are crushed in spirit (Psalm 38:14, NIV)". He delivered me from my brokenhearted emptiness, so that I can share His goodness and mercy with His children. This was my "attention getter" moment from God. We all have one. **Have you experienced yours yet? If not, please know, this time is coming.** This experience served as my time to "Get Up!" by the man whom I had spent so many years chasing behind and hiding from God from.

I had devoted so much time to a man who did not see my value. I spent years being berated and told that I "wasn't enough"; I hid myself from God. I know now that even when we think we are hiding He is still watching and waiting for us to return to Him. God slowly began to reveal to me the origins of all the heartache, anger, loneliness, and sadness.

While going through these days of feeling lonely, sad, mad, and lacking self-esteem because I had been told, "I wasn't enough"by the man whom I had spent so many years chasing behind and hiding from God from. I had devoted so much time to a man who made me feel like nothing. I spent years being berated and told that I "wasn't enough"; I hid myself from God. I know now that even when we think we are hiding He is still watching and waiting for us to return to Him. God slowly began to reveal to me the origins of all the heartache, anger, loneliness, and sadness.

One day, God started showing me the many different things I had experienced and witnessed throughout my life going back to my childhood. Here I was in my forties, mother of two and grandmother of two yet I was starting to relive my years of molestation which happened from around four years old until about age 10 or 11. It started at such an early age and happened so often. The years are now faint because of the mental block I had put up.

It began when I was around four years old and persisted until I was ten or eleven. Though it is difficult for me to recall exactly when it occurred, because I had mentally blocked out the encounter. Nevertheless, I was very young when it began, and it went on for quite some time over my childhood. Thank God for discernment. I understood these thoughts and I did not allow it to make my depression worse. **See ladies, you have to be careful and know if your thoughts are from God or the enemy, because Satan is very tempting.** He studies us well and has no problem devouring those of us who are not built up in Christ with strength and wisdom. Choosing to listen to Satan will lead us to the path right to hell. Whereas, knowing that God needs us to be by following His commands. It becomes our daily language and movement.

Satan is extremely sly and tempting. It is imperative that you study the Word of God so that you will not be fooled by Satan's attempts to distort God's message. This will also help you to surrender control to God with peace in knowing that you are exactly where He needs you to be. You must follow His commands daily in all aspects of your life. That is not to say that you won't fall short sometimes; however, you must make an active decision to turn to Him in those times.

THE SHIFT

I began to shift my focus from the heartbreak and hurt to forgiveness instead. I started to understand God's intent. To move on in life I needed to forgive those who hurt and rejected me in the past. Yes, this included the person who molested me and the man who broke my heart. Funny thing is, I didn't even realize how much of my childhood had affected what I had become as an adult. It did! My life was greatly impacted by the past. It caused me to not show up being the mother that my kids often needed. Hell, I wasn't even sure if I was showing up for me when I needed to. Doing drugs, dealing drugs, hanging with the wrong crowds to fit in, being promiscuous, and allowing what others had to say to me or about me dictate my character was the kind of life I was living. For many years, I was a complete mess. Falling in and out of depression. Every spiritual yoke that was attached. I had to lose. If I hadn't of, I might not be here to tell this story. As a matter of fact, God already told me that. If I hadn't chosen to follow Jesus as my commander, I'd be dead or in jail.

During the time I was reliving my childhood trauma, I'm grateful that I understood what God was doing. I couldn't help but to shed tears because no child should have experienced what I did. The sick sexual behaviors I experienced were not normal! My emotions were all over the place as I recalled these actions. Each time I wanted to get angry at something that happened over 20 years ago, God would step in and show me that it was all necessary. The only thing that gave me a resemblance of peace was forgiving them. You see, during this time my thoughts ran rampant! Scenes from the past kept replaying in my head. Years of molestation! What about the time my great uncle touched me as a kid while my grandparents sat close by drinking and I was too ashamed to tell anyone. Now that I think about it, maybe I was scared. Fear kept my mouth closed.

You may be asking why I would be fearful. Why wouldn't I tell an adult what was happening when this uncle sat me on his lap. Maybe it was because I was warned that telling would cause trouble in the family. Maybe I was scared that telling would cause my dad to go to prison. I didn't want my dad in jail because for twelve years (all before I turned 18), my dad had been in and out of local jails and state penitentiaries. I couldn't be the cause of him going back. God had me thinking about all of this. God continued to show how He had been with me my *entire* life. I spent so many years verbally saying how I had forgiven my dad for not being around and for the many years of imprisonment. I got so used to him not being around. I had convinced myself that his lengthy jail time did not bother me. I had been fooling myself all these years.

Reflecting over my life as I write this story showed me how broken I was. This is why I spent so many years looking for love in all the wrong places. I wanted attention from any man that would give me time. I preferred the attention of "bad boys" because they reminded me of my father. I encountered nice boys, but that wasn't my preference. I settled in most relationships and I was treated as such. I did not know my worth because as a young woman, I was still mentally the little girl waiting for her father to show up. The mental bondage didn't stop there.

For many years in my childhood, I witnessed my mom partying and putting her fun before me. These recalled moments seemed less traumatic because while it was disturbing, my love for my momma overshadowed it all. It may make no sense and may not be right, but I know my mom loved me. I honestly don't think my momma knew how to show me love. I believe my mom was suppressing her own emotional traumas of generational drinking and drugs. Her activities meant she wasn't always available for me. This meant my grandmothers had to step in and raise me. I tried talking to my mom as part of the healing process because I truly wanted healing as a family. These conversations were difficult and sometimes resulted in us clashing with each other. I had to be the one to understand the bigger picture. My lesson in this and something I'll share with you is: **Your parents loved you the way they knew how.**

I kept trying to figure out God's message to me. He was revealing so much to me about my family, that even as I type this, my family still doesn't know. This period of revelation wasn't for my family. It was for me to sit with, forgive, then begin the journey of healing. Again, forgiveness has been my peace. I forgave the man who raped me in my late 20's. I forgave the great uncle who touched me inappropriately as a young girl. I forgave every guy who took advantage of my heart and body. I even forgave those people who counted me out. Most importantly, I forgave myself. I was harboring inner emotions that became spiritual yokes and bondage.

Over the course of two years, I sat in a spiritual waiting room. I needed to discover who I was and whose I was. God would have me settle with my restoration season by healing from my internal wounds. Not only did healing begin during this time, but I found my voice. Being vocal about my truths allowed me to help heal many others. My life story became an open book for those who know me, or those who are members of my Facebook platform, "Girl, give Me Your Hand." Life has thrown many obstacles my way, and if you're reading this, maybe it's thrown some your way too. I'm now thankful for every experience. What the enemy thought was going to destroy me has given me the push to become a better version of myself.

Please understand ladies, this means every day I have to work and renew my mind. My only competition is myself. I will never sleep on me again or allow anyone else to.

My attention is now focused on my Savior–Jesus, the Christ! I'm up now, holding His hand. Not only did I get up holding His hand, but I plan to help others get up by holding their hands!

Five Tips while in The Waiting Room

1. We must be active in prayer in our waiting!

   Just as David said in Psalms 5:1-2 "Give ear to my words, O Lord, consider my meditation. Hearken unto the voice of my cry, my King, and my God: for unto thee will I pray."

   Pray in thanks, repentance, or in petition to the Lord to hear your prayers. God shall bring us through.

2. Surrender to God's timing and Plan in the Waiting Room!

   As humans, surrendering is hard, because we like to be in control. We like to control how and when things will happen; not being in control makes us feel uncomfortable and unsafe.

   "Trust in the Lord with all your heart; do not depend on your own understanding. Seek His will in all you do, and He will show you which path to take." Proverbs 3:5-6

3. Identity, identity, identity…Remember Whose you are!

   During your waiting season, you will feel more desperate, vulnerable, and uncomfortable than ever before. It is essential for this reason that you self-affirm daily by confessing the verse(s) that God spoke about us:

   "She is clothed with strength and dignity, and she laughs without fear of the future." Proverbs 31:25 NLT

4. Read the Bible while waiting!

Stay in scripture, especially in seasons of waiting. Often what feels like waiting is really a season of preparation. It may be that our heart needs some work or it may be that God is moving in other areas to prepare the way.

"For everything that was written in the past was written
to teach us so that through the endurance taught in the
Scriptures and the encouragement they provide we might
have hope." Romans 15:4

5. Surrender to the will while you wait!

Change is a process and can take time. When God is working a change in your life or carrying you through a particular challenge, it may take time. Do not fight the process, surrender to God's work in your heart, and Submit to God's timing/process. Let go of your attempts to control and plan your way out of the will of God. Allow God to lead.

"Commit your way to the LORD; trust in him and he will do
this: He will make your righteous reward shine like the dawn,
your vindication like the noonday sun. Be still before the
LORD and wait patiently for him; do not fret when people
succeed in their ways, when they carry out their wicked
schemes. Refrain from anger and turn from wrath; do not
fret—it leads only to evil. For those who are evil will be
destroyed, but those who hope in the LORD will inherit the
land." Psalm 37:5-9 NIV

Acknowledgments

I would like to thank Debbie Carter, the Visionary of this book, for believing in me enough to push this version of my testimony out. I would like to thank my daughter for being my motivation and push to share my story. My husband, for being supportive of all of my dreams and goals.

And to everyone who believed in me and to those who didn't: You all helped me to see what God has seen in me all along, someone with purpose!

Now, I've been Positioned into Purpose for His glory. I humbly say, "Thank You!"

Dedication

I'm dedicating this chapter to my Daughter T'Kāla. I pray that you find your healing and deliverance in your personal battles. I pray that your light is never too dull for you to find Jesus while you wait on your breakthrough. Know that I will forever love you, stand with you, and that I share my stories so that others may find their healing. My prayer is that others can have insight on how to approach the attacks of the enemy because of my testimonials, and most importantly to break the generational curses and bondage that has been put on the woman in our family.

Decree and Declare with me …. "Our family curses are broken! So that Jakye & Ayahna will be whole!"

Reflections

_____
_____
_____
_____
_____
_____
_____
_____
_____
_____
_____
_____
_____
_____
_____
_____
_____
_____
_____
_____

Reflections

Reflections

CHAPTER

IV

The Overcomer
(STORMS COME BUT THE SUN SHINES AGAIN)

LATOSHA L. VENEY

Latosha L. Veney is a woman of many hats and talents. Her life's journey consists of running the daily operations of a home care agency, being partner of another home care agency, a medical staffing agency, life coaching, consulting, and inspiring others through her words as an author and speaker. Because of her ability to effectively and compassionately serve the elderly and home care communities, one of her home care businesses received the "Best in Newport News" in 2019. As a consultant, Latosha is passionate about teaching new home care business owners the knowledge that she has acquired over the years. She also believes in the importance of individuals reaching their full potential. Through her certified life coaching program and motivational speaking, she provides others with practical tools, strategies and daily resources to ensure growth when applied. Latosha is the author of My Quiet Storm and How to Quiet Your Storm. Her purpose for writing these books was to share an account of the storms she has overcome in her life in hopes of empowering others to quiet their own "storms."

When she is not changing the world, she is traveling, reading, and creating lasting moments with her family.

Have you ever been in love?

I mean, truly in love. I am talking about that "knock you off your feet, I can't breathe without you " type of love. The love that makes you want to stay up all night because you can't imagine being able to sleep without hearing their voice. The love that makes you forget about all the people who came before them. The love that pushes you to let your guard down and open your heart because this is *The One*.

As with anything new, there is always excitement in the air and you wonder: Where did this man come from? Why me?

My excitement brought on the same questions. Yet, what alerted my anxiety was the fact that he told me that he had just been released from jail for a murder charge that he didn't commit. The charge was thrown out. Though I had my reservations, I continued to get to know him because he did tell me about his past when he didn't have to reveal it. My mother is one of my best friends, so I felt it was necessary to share his past with her. I valued her wisdom and truth. After speaking to her, we both agreed that people make poor choices at times. Many people learn from those poor choices and seek changes. Something about this man intrigued me, and I truly wanted to get to know him.

We continued to date. I felt comfortable and safe. He was always concerned about my feelings, constantly asking if I was okay. We were opposites, but that didn't matter to me. He frequently called me "sheltered." I must admit that I was in that season of my life. Because I had isolated myself, I wasn't able to develop many friendships. Honestly, mingling hadn't been a priority for me. I was oblivious to what was happening in the outside world. He was on the other end of the spectrum. He was social, a people person, always willing to talk to anyone. I was the sheltered one and I called him the "hood" one, yet, we were both okay with the reality of our personalities. We didn't care about them clashing because being together overrode any feelings of uncertainty or red flags.

Life has a way of surprising you with unexplainable twists and turns. I had amazing dreams for my new love and new family. Being able to say that I bounced back after a disastrous divorce was imperative to me. At first things were all that I had imagined. We were growing and learning from each other. We were becoming. Despite the previous obstacles, I was confident that my Love and I would get through any other hell that came our way. Unfortunately, there would come a day that shook and turned my world upside down.

I remember waking up one morning, ready to attack the day. Business and life were awesome, and my confidence grew every time I set foot into my office. That morning, I was encouraged by my future goals and the return of my business investments. I didn't have a care in the world. There were some errands that I had to run that morning and as always, I left my employees to accomplish their tasks at hand. Having a loyal and competent team was one of my business blessings. While running my errands, I checked back in to make sure that things were running smoothly and to see if anyone wanted a lunch pickup. Unfortunately, no one answered any of the phone lines. I even tried calling their individual cell phones–the response was still the same. Alarmed, I began to wonder if we had been bombarded with a surprise inspection. Though things were in order, I knew how a surprise inspection could cause anxiety and friction throughout the office, especially with the boss not being there.

Suddenly, my cell phone rang. It was the office. To my surprise, I was notified that I needed to return back to the office immediately. Even after questioning the reason for the rush, the answers weren't readily available. Not a soul was able to articulate what was happening in my business over the phone. As I rushed down the highway, a plethora of thoughts entered my mind. I couldn't fathom what could have warranted the reason for the frenzy in my office. A few hours earlier, all was right with the world. My business and life were flourishing. How could something suddenly alter that truth in such a short period of time? To my disbelief, something had been brewing for quite some time.

Upon arriving at my office, I found the parking lot completely full. This was odd because, other than a few of my typical employees, the parking lot was usually empty. My heart was beating in suspense and fear. What was going on? Determined to find out the truth, I rushed to the elevator. As I hopped on to the elevator, ignoring the rush of individuals who zoomed past me, I noticed that two men joined me. We made eye contact. Eventually, one of the gentlemen said my name and showed me a picture. To my surprise, it was a picture of my new Love. I was asked if I was aware of the man in the picture. I confidently stated that the man in the picture was my fiancé. Immediately, I felt worried. Was he hurt? What did these gentlemen want with the man of my dreams? What I was hit with next blew my mind and changed my world.

The gentlemen let me know that the reason for the intrusion in my office was because my fiancé was a suspect in a drug conspiracy. To say I was shocked would be an understatement–I was floored . My fiancé's behavior had brought the drug task force to my establishment. I couldn't believe it! This further proved my belief that connections matter. Your connections can either make or break you. I was oblivious to his dealings because I had been so focused on his love and rebuilding my relationship image. There had to have been signs that would have shown what he had been up to. How did I miss this? Is love truly blind?

I knew that my business had the propensity of being tainted from this news–since a drug conspiracy wasn't the best look and could have disastrous outcomes. The officers informed me that my space would be overtaken by dogs and individuals trying to get their jobs done. I tried to prepare myself for this invasion of privacy. Still in disbelief, I kindly asked about my staff. To my delight, my staff were okay and still in the office.

I couldn't understand why my office was being searched. Was I a suspect in this ordeal? Fortunately not, but because of my connection to him, I was a person of interest. The officers stated that my office was being searched because my fiancé had been seen coming and going from the office. It was important for the drug task force to see if drugs were being smuggled in and out of my space.

IS THIS REALLY HAPPENING?

I couldn't believe that this was happening to me. I wasn't perfect, but I tried my hardest to be a person that was compassionate to others, helpful and deserving of God's best. With tears in my eyes, I watched as my office was being searched and scrutinized all because of whom I loved. My office manager, a praying lady, remained calm through the search. She held and consoled me as I cried. The other staff members sat in disbelief, many with teary eyes as well. This was a shock to us all. The time seemed to drag on and I wondered where my children and my fiancé were located. The officers informed me that my children were safe but my fiancé had been taken into custody. As the hours passed, the search seemed to be never ending. The questions continued. All the cash that I had in my office that needed to be deposited was taken. When my cell phone rang, they took that too. It seemed as if I was a prisoner in my own establishment. At around 8 p.m., we were released from the confines of my office but not after being told how long I had been watched. For six months, my routines had been monitored by the police. They knew my coming and going. They knew what I did from sunup to sundown. I had never felt so violated in my life. And this was birthed out of love? No, this couldn't be love.

For a quick second, I thought about that love. I reflected on our happy times in disbelief. Was it even real? As I stared around my office, I wanted to believe that my fiancé had a logical answer for disrupting my life in this manner. My heart yearned for the truth. There had to be a valid reason for his actions. I wasn't sure when I would receive those answers, but my mind wouldn't allow me to dwell on it. Finding my children and getting things back in order took precedence over hearing from my fiancé. When the authorities finally released us, I hurried home. Unfortunately, I found an even bigger mess at my residence. A search had been done within my home as well. My place of solace had been flipped upside down. If it hadn't been for my sister and my brother-in-law, I knew that I wouldn't have been able to make it through that entire ordeal. They cleaned things up and put my house back in order as my heart shattered into pieces. That night, I remember praying and praying some more. I was hurt, broken, and unsure of what to do next. Things had to go back to normal, and God had to show up.

Later that night, I heard from my fiancé. The authorities had informed us earlier regarding the severity of his crimes. I desperately needed to understand how the man I loved could have put his family in such a serious bind. At 2 a.m., I heard his distraught voice. He lamented on how he had gotten caught up. He tried to update me on what had occurred and why. All I wanted to do at that moment was strangle him through the phone. How dare he put me and the kids through this foolishness? Then he explained that he would be gone for a very long time. I listened in disbelief. And just like that, my fiance was gone–this wasn't the life that I had signed up for.

It is amazing how you can make plans and have a whole picture regarding your life. Everything can be laid out so well. Then suddenly, tragedy, unforeseen circumstances, or the bad judgment of others can destroy your pretty picture. I felt as if I was in the twilight zone. "How would I explain this to my kids?" I wondered. There was still so much left unsaid, and it was as if my fiancé wasn't sharing the whole story. Eventually, the phone call ended, leaving me broken and unsure. That night I couldn't sleep. Like clockwork, I was up every night until 2 a.m., filled with sadness and anxiety. The attacks were horrendous. My life was in shambles and my emotional state wasn't that far behind.

During this season, the thoughts of moving played in my head. I was afraid of who my fiancé knew and whether they would come looking for him. What if they thought he had money and decided to rob me? Who knew where I lived? Was I truly safe? My kids' safety was imperative. To ease my troubled mind, I made the decision to change residences. I couldn't afford to take any chances. It wasn't just my wellbeing that I had to focus on. I had my children plus my niece and nephew to raise and doing it alone wasn't the plan. My fiancé and I were supposed to be on this journey together. What was I going to do?

Fortunately, I found a new home in a quiet area. Adjusting was difficult. I found myself sinking into a depression. There wasn't any desire to do anything. Eating, washing and functioning outside of the home wasn't important. Most days, the kids kept me grounded. The more that I heard about my fiancé's dealings, the worse my worry became. It was time to hire an attorney, especially because I needed the money back that the officials took. I wanted to know why they stated that I was safe, for now. What did that mean? Were they continuously monitoring my every move? I needed answers. Most importantly, I needed to feel safe and secure.

It didn't matter what I shared with them. They refused to believe my truth. I hated to leave the house because it seemed as if I was constantly being followed. Every time I went into my office, I was constantly being reminded of this horrible season and my fiancé's poor choices. Not being able to truly escape this fiasco affected me mentally, physically, spiritually, emotionally and financially. This heavy burden held me in bondage and refused to release me. It impacted my everyday life. I wasn't present. I wasn't in tune with anything. Though things were happening around me, I felt invisible and lost. This wasn't life and this wasn't God's plan for me. I knew that a change needed to happen, but I wasn't sure how to break out of my trance.

THE RAFT

One day, a lady came into the office and told me a story about her friend. Her friend had stopped coming to work and isolated herself from those who loved her. No one was able to reach her. Eventually, they decided to go to her house. They were greeted with darkness and found their friend, lying there lifeless but still alive. She was severely depressed and had given up on life. She hadn't bathed or dressed. As I listened to this woman tell her friend's story, I saw so many similarities. I knew I was in trouble. If I didn't get out of this funk, I was going to be the same way. I made the decision to go home and take back my life. I opened my blinds. I let the light in. While cleaning up, I prayed to God, asking Him to give me the strength needed to fight these demons and despair. I realized that waking up at 2 a.m. for prayer with Mrs. V was too much. I had to get my anxiety under control. Self-care was necessary and I poured into the self-help books readily available. The determination that I had lost started to resurface. Positive affirmations kept me grounded. It helped to remind me that I wasn't at fault. Regardless of how criminal the officials made me feel, I didn't do anything wrong. Things would get better and I was sure of it.

My fiance's sentencing took about a year's time. Throughout the process, we did communicate, but it was limited. I remained focused on my system of self-care and started to regain my life. The day of sentencing came and I was filled with much dread. I didn't want to have a relapse and didn't want to participate in the negativity of the court system. I finally got to a place of peace and didn't want anything to disrupt that. Fortunately, I had an amazing support system. The day of court, my mom, sister and nephew came along. My two prayer warriors, Mrs. V and Mrs. Y were also present. Everyone knew that my fiancé had made a terrible decision that impacted the lives of so many yet he had some good characteristics still in him.

As I sat in that Federal court, I immediately felt uneasy. The whole experience was frightening. On one side of the courtroom were a lot of young people brought there through a program to show them the truth about life and what could occur if they didn't improve their lives.

Eventually, my fiancé entered the courtroom. I wasn't prepared for the feelings of heartbreak that surfaced. I wanted to immediately flee, but something kept me in my seat. As the sentencing proceedings continued, I learned so much about my fiancé. I listened and realized that I hadn't truly known him at all. The things that people should discuss during dating hadn't been discussed. I knew nothing about his childhood or his drug-addicted mother. I didn't know that his mother taught him to do drugs at age seven or that he smoked weed with his mom for the first time at age six. I was shocked to hear these things, especially since I am a mother.

My fiancé was taught how to rob in order to survive. The life of the street was all that he knew. Though he saw the life he had with me as a blessing, he didn't know how to function in it. He always reverted to what he knew. The learned behavior took over. Everyone in the courtroom sat in disbelief. My fiancé's upbringing left us all flabbergasted.

That was the last time that I saw my fiancé outside of the penitentiary. At that moment, I was forced to start over.

DARKNESS TO LIGHT

Depression came in like a world wind. Like a storm that was totally out of my control. Depression and I had a great thing going. We were lazy together. We shared the same mindset. We sulked around the house together. When I was down, depression was down. When I wanted to give up, depression wanted to give up. When I was blinded by my emotions, depression was blind as well. We made the perfect pair. Though I knew that I had to break free from its hold, I wasn't ready. I found comfort in wallowing. Doing nothing was unusually calming. Typically, I had the drive and determination as a stallion. When depression was around, lying around the stable was fine with me.

What I learned during this season was that depression was a tactic of the enemy to keep me bound. As long as I was depressed, I couldn't move forward. Depression sat on my chest, taking away my energy and at times the ability to breath. I was stuck. Thankfully, my support system wouldn't let me stay there.

Though the storm that I endured quietly crept in on me, I couldn't allow it to halt what I knew God was trying to do in my life. Remember, everything that we go through is purposeful. The traumas we face do not negate the assignment on our lives. Losing my fiance to crime and prison time could not erase the fact that I had been created for a great purpose. One that God still expected me to fulfill.

Starting over was necessary. It goes hand and in hand with healing. Starting over required me to change my mindset about what I wanted my life to look like and refocus on what God wanted it to look like. It first began with my spiritual journey. The woman that you see today is because of my relationship with God and His keeping power. If it weren't for Him, I wouldn't have made it. God gave me the strength to keep going when I wanted to give up. When I didn't think that I had what it took to raise my kids, niece and nephew alone, God showed me why and how I could. I am not a religious woman, but I am a spiritual one. I can revere God because He was with me and I watched Him bring me out of one of my toughest journeys.

Everything about life is better because of this important relationship. I am not perfect, yet He loves me anyway. I fall short and He continues to call on me. I have learned how to depend on Him wholeheartedly. Putting God first has helped me choose the best friendships and business connections. I did have my questions about why He allowed me to go through that season that almost broke me. The reality is that it didn't break me. Though it hurt, I am still here. God makes no mistakes. He is the head and with Him leading, I have nothing to worry about.

Because of my relationship with God, I feel stronger than ever. I am going back to church more often. The relationship with my ex affected me in a negative way, drawing me away from God. I didn't realize it until I was out of the situation. It is amazing what is revealed when you are no longer distracted. I learned so much about the reasons behind why I connected myself to this man. He was totally different from my first husband yet I was drawn to him. Maybe it was the swag or the fun of it all. Nonetheless, I learned that I had rushed into that relationship. I should have taken my time and asked the right questions. He shouldn't have met my daughter until I was sure of his background. If I had taken my time, I would have learned about his childhood and how that could disastrously affect our future together. I wasn't focused on taking my time. The great feelings of belonging that he gave me seemed to override my better judgment. My unwillingness to make the right decision in this, caused me to suffer through a season of depression. I was impatient and a little desperate for my daughter to have a father-figure in her life. Through it all, and dealing with fear and anxiety from my encounters with the police, I am so grateful that God gives us beauty for ashes.

Women, we must be diligent about looking for the signs. You know what those signs, or red flags are. It is imperative for our wellbeing. Desperation breeds disaster. When we are too focused on being loved and appreciated, we tend to miss important steps and indications that prove that the person we are pursuing or who is pursuing us may not be the right person. God will reveal a person's true colors. We just must be ready to see them.

Don't feel like God is going to leave you out. Every person or thing that you are supposed to be connected to will be yours. There's nothing that you can do that will stop God from fulfilling His plan for your life. He knows how to guide you through every detour. He is skilled at making beautiful things out of messes. When you submit to His will, beginning again will be a smooth process. Even through the bumps of life, you will be able to glide through without a hitch. God has the remedy for every issue, every illness, every heartbreak, and every wrong turn. With Him, beginning again is the safest and most rewarding thing that we will do in our lifetime.

To My Readers:

I don't have 5 Tips to help you in The Waiting Room, but I will say this, *Don't allow life's circumstances deter you from walking in boldness. The storms will come. Stay Steadfast. You will overcome them.*

Dedication

TO MY READERS:

Life has had its ups and downs but I am here to say, "This too shall pass." It does get better and you can start over fresh. I wrote this as a way to encouarge others while they are in their Waiting Room. The truth is that sometimes it is hard to bounce back after a storm. Sometimes, the waiting knocks us out. Though the wait may seem brutal our wait may have the propensity to change the trajectory of our life story. Everything hard doesn't necessarily have to be washed away as hard. Hard doesn't have to have negative connotations. Hard can be good–the wait can be good!

Right now, as you sit and read these words, I want you to reflect on your "waiting seasons." What did the wait teach you/what is it teaching you? Are you a better woman because of it? Even though you didn't eagerly invite these tribulations, they did play a part in your becoming who you are today.

Embrace each challenging moment because they are sure to come. Understand that you are equipped to handle each drop of rain that falls unexpectedly. Great things takes place as we wait.

Reflections

_____

_____

_____

_____

_____

_____

_____

_____

_____

_____

_____

_____

_____

_____

_____

_____

_____

_____

_____

_____

_____

Reflections

Reflections

CHAPTER

V

Hope for completion exists IN THE DOCTORAL WAITING ROOM

DR. KEIMA SHERIFF

Dr. Keima Sheriff, Dean of Holistic Support at Montgomery County Community College, has over 20 years of professional experience as an educator, program director, and administrator. Dr. Sheriff joined Montgomery County Community College in 2013 to launch and lead the Gateway to College Program. Under her seven-years of leadership, the program has experienced several local and national programmatic successes. Teaching Adolescent Psychology, Dr. Sheriff also serves as adjunct faculty at Montgomery County College. Dr. Sheriff founded the organizational management consulting firm, Dr. Kem Speaks (formerly the Institute for Balance and Restoration). The organization strives to identify and cultivate sustainable organizational, leadership and employee resiliency for academic institutions, corporate and non-profit business.

Dr. Sheriff has served as a consultant to several human service, education, and youth development programs in Philadelphia and the surrounding suburbs. In her consultation role, she worked on significant projects like the development of the Pennsylvania Keystone Stars with the United Way of Southeastern Pennsylvania and establishing the truancy partnership between the Department of Human Services, Philadelphia School District, and the Philadelphia Family Court system. She received a

Bachelor of Arts degree for the combined study of Psychology and Political Science at Albright College in 1996, and has earned a Master of Social Service in program planning, development, and analysis from Bryn Mawr College in 2003. Dr. Sheriff received her Doctorate in Higher Education from Immaculata University in January 2019. Her dissertation, Finishing in Faith: An Autoethnographic Exploration of the Intersection of Faith and Doctoral Program Completion, examined how Black, Christian women applied their faith as a persistence strategy to complete their doctoral programs. She hopes to use this research to advance strength-based research and completion initiatives to support higher education program completion.

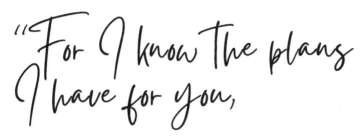

declares the LORD, plans to prosper you and not to harm you,

plans to give you hope and a future"

(Jeremiah 29:11, Holy Bible: New International Version)

MY ELEVEN-YEAR DOCTORAL JOURNEY IS CAPTURED IN THE FOLLOWING 19 SENTENCES:

A Black woman. First generation doctoral student.

Single parent of a young son. Student

loan debt twice my total mortgage and rising.

Crisis of confidence. Two-year writing paralysis.

Health challenges. Launching a new consulting practice with

several clients. The recession.

Leaner budgets meant losing all but two clients.

Transition from full time consulting to full time

employment in higher education. Imposter Syndrome.

A marriage. A divorce. A personal

financial crisis. Eleven years pursuing my doctorate.

wo different doctoral programs.

Deep levels of fatigue. Yet, hope persists….

When we step into our dream or goal pursuit, we enter a space filled with immense opportunity and potential. Pregnant with hope and excitement, we focus on the outcome, not the journey. However, it is the richness of the journey, the Waiting Room of ups and downs, that informs how we can work our way through life. This eleven-year doctoral pursuit taught me that the journey is far more important than achieving the desired outcome. This doctoral journey was, without question, my most difficult dream pursuit to date. It was marked by a volatile combination of joy, disappointment, excitement, scholarship, enjoyment, resentment, loss, gain, desperation, and hope. The tumultuous experience caused me to reflect many times on how I persisted from the September 2007 doctoral program starting line to fighting for a 2018 finish line. The above scripture verse served as my source of hope during dark and overwhelming days. I believed that no matter how difficult this process was, I would achieve successful completion. In what was a vibrant, exciting, and complicated doctoral labyrinth, this verse served as my beacon during times when the maze seemed to lead me to impossible obstacles, blocked passages, and endless missteps.

As a woman of strong faith, I believe God knows the plans He has for me and they are to prosper me, never to harm me; to give me hope and an amazing future. Despite the many painful trials and potentially derailing experiences, I believed God will bring me to my expected prosperous end: completing my doctoral program. But how could I know, with absolute certainty, I would complete my program? How could I, a Black, Christian woman, representing a marginalized, under-resourced student population, be assured I would complete the doctoral program when the statistics for doctoral program completion says otherwise? Even more confounding, how could I still believe that I would complete the program knowing I timed-out of my first program and would have to start over somewhere else to complete my degree?

Pushing past major obstacles and trials in pursuit of my doctorate, I have repeatedly reflected on my ability to persist to completion. As the years progressed, I witnessed many other women, especially Black women, with similar or greater challenges pursue and complete their doctoral programs. I have also witnessed colleagues who were facing major academic and personal difficulties make what they considered one of the most difficult decisions in their lives, which was to leave their programs before completion. Despite strongly considering walking away prior to completion as some of my colleagues did, what made me persist? As a life-long learner, I have always been a hard working, capable, and successful student. Even though it was the scariest decision of my life, I decided to shift the socioeconomic path for my family by leaving home to become a first-generation college student in pursuit of a Bachelor's Degree. While it was true that I negotiated challenges during my undergraduate and graduate programs, I never doubted my ability to persist and successfully complete those programs.

Unlike my previous experiences, my strong sense of self-efficacy (my belief that I could be successful) and my belief in my academic abilities were not enough to keep me fully engaged in completing my doctoral degree. I fought to stay academically engaged in a way that I have never experienced during my entire higher education journey. What made this degree significantly more challenging to complete than my previous degrees? What was fueling my desire to complete this program?

This personal inquiry served as the foundation for my dissertation. The study, borne out of my doctoral experiences, is an exploration of how Black, Christian women who, in pursuit of doctoral program completion, relied on their religious faith during "Job Moments" to persist to completion. For the purpose of the study, I adapted the biblical story of Job and his unyielding faith in God despite the great adversity he endured (Holy Bible, 2011). As the Bible recounts, Job–wealthy, righteous, deeply faithful, and well-favored by many–was allowed to experience a series of trials, lasting several months but no more than a year, to demonstrate that his faith in God was not based on the protection and many blessings God had given him, but instead, was based on an unyielding belief and faith in the sovereign wisdom of God. Job was stripped of all his material possessions and family (his animals, servants and children were killed when the building they were in collapsed), excellent health (he was stricken with sores all over his body), and his high status in the community. His wife turned against him and chastised him for still believing in God despite what had befallen him and urged him to curse God and go die. Three of his good friends came to be with and comfort him during his trials and in speaking with him began believing that perhaps Job was really a bad man deserving of his punishment. Believing himself to be righteous and without sin, Job insisted he was undeserving of the calamities that befell him. He wrestled emotionally with the conflict of believing himself to be righteous yet being made to suffer for no apparent reason. Job judged himself to be righteous rather than acknowledge his righteousness was a result of God's righteousness. Although reverent and within the framework of a faithful and obedient servant to God, Job questioned God about the level of suffering he, a righteous man, was being made to endure.

God became angry with Job's friends for accusing him of being a bad person without just cause or evidence. Job prayed to God to forgive his friends and God answered his prayers. God then spoke to Job, asking him a series of questions that profoundly shifted and expanded his perspective on how God moves in the lives of His people. The three key questions God asked Job were, "Where were you when I laid the foundation of the earth?" (Holy Bible, Job 38:4). Followed by, "Have you ever in your days commanded the morning light?" (Holy Bible, Job 38:12). And finally, "Where does light live, or where does darkness reside?" (Holy Bible, Job 38:19). In that moment, Job realized how immensely unfathomable God's power, wisdom, and authority are compared to his extremely limited existence. At that, Job atoned for his previously held beliefs and developed an even deeper understanding of God's sovereignty in the universe and in the lives of His children. God then restored everything that was taken from Job, twice as much as he once had (Holy Bible, 2011). Even with all the obstacles and challenges he endured; Job never lost faith in God's divine wisdom and authority over his life. The three key lessons learned from Job's experience of and survival through hardships: 1) pray for others even if they wrong you; 2) maintain your righteousness by not letting your circumstances cause you to behave in a way that is out of alignment with God's will for your life (i.e. do not allow your trials to cause you to disobey God); and 3) never lose faith in God's goodness or the hope that He will get you through your trials.

Although the biblical story of Job is commonly referred to as a source of hope when one is facing a particularly difficult season, a literature search for non-religious applications did not reveal any scholarly or academic interpretations. Based on the challenges experienced in pursuit of my doctorate, I am personally able to identify with the story of Job. Prior to entering my doctoral program, I appreciated significant levels of academic success. Despite being a strong and capable student, for reasons beyond my control or comprehension, I endured several trials that caused me to question my very purpose (and ability) for pursuing the degree. I resonated strongly with Job's unyielding determination to remain committed to his faith and belief that God's mercy would prevail. For this reason, I coined the phrase "Job Moment" to highlight the significance of both the trials I and the other study participants faced and the depth of our faith in God to help us overcome those trials in pursuit of degree completion. For my dissertation, Job Moments were defined as those times the participants faced significant adversity that caused them to consider leaving or temporarily left their programs but later decided to return and persist in the pursuit of program completion. Specifically, my autoethnographic study was an attempt to explore the lived experiences of Black, Christian women doctoral students in our active and intentional reliance on our faith and how that reliance supported the development of our resilience to move beyond barriers to pursue and for the women to achieve academic completion.

Through this autoethnographic study, as both researcher and participant, I was offered the opportunity to include my personal experiences as a Black, woman, doctoral student who was able to persist in pursuit of academic completion despite experiencing several Job Moments. In essence, the researcher serves as both researcher and participant. That is, despite the existing deficit-based research focused on the high attrition rates of marginalized and underrepresented graduate students- the nature and rigor of my autoethnographic study provided voice to and value for the lived experiences of Black women in the pursuit of, and for many, the successful completion of their doctoral programs.

The study was an effort to support other researchers who are working to shift the narrative of a deficit-based to a strengths-based perspective when examining the lived experiences of marginalized communities. Rather than focusing on the factors that prohibit academic completion (deficit-based), my dissertation was interested in understanding what strategies support doctoral program persistence and completion (strengths-based). In that respect, the exploration shifts the focus from examining deficits to embracing what I and the participants consider a strength. Social science researchers and practitioners have shifted their approach to supporting human development from one of deficit-based thinking (diagnosing or focusing on the problem) to a strengths-based approach (identifying and validating what individuals consider their strengths). People from marginalized and oppressed-lived experiences learn how to make do with the little they may have access to, to create what they need to survive and, hopefully, one day, thrive. Strengths-based research looks at these survival skills and embraces them as a demonstration of resilience. I see our dependence on God as a demonstration of strength and a way to move beyond surviving and into thriving. For the purposes of my dissertation, Black women who believed our active reliance on our Christian faith supported our ability to persist in our graduate program was explored as a strength in the pursuit of doctoral program completion. That is, exploring the strength of how God worked on, with, through and for us while we waited in the Waiting Room to get to program completion. The findings of my dissertation, when used in conjunction with other strength-based studies, can help shift the design of deficit-based research questions from focusing on why Black women specifically, and perhaps the marginalized generally, have lower educational achievement attainment when compared to White students. Instead, future studies can reframe the interest in understanding how these students are able to excel academically and complete their programs despite the cultural, social, political, and economic challenges they encounter. Additionally, my dissertation can encourage graduate program administrators to consider ways they can expand their student support services to include opportunities for students to intentionally integrate their faith as a part of their support services programming. Finally, it is hoped that my study can build a bridge between academia and faith-based communities by demonstrating the importance of having a comprehensive, supportive community in whole student development and academic completion.

In addition to expanding the conversation to consider the strategies marginalized cultures employ to achieve academic completion, it is also important to note other positive impacts their completion will have on higher education. For instance, greater numbers of ethnic minorities who are able to complete doctoral programs will create an opportunity to address the severe underrepresentation of minorities in the professorship. Having increased ethnic representation can pave the way for a holistic learning environment by providing diversity of thought, perception, and experiences. A more diverse professorship also increases mentorship opportunities for students of color. In turn, more students of color may consider becoming a part of the academy because they see diversity among the faculty.

The study revealed several promising, applicable tactics to support academic completion. Not surprising, we all reported high levels of self-efficacy with academic mastery/confidence being our highest sense of efficacy followed by having a positive emotional state and ability to compartmentalize potential barriers. In addition to our individual sense of self-efficacy, we reported having supportive advising relationships and participation in cohort groups as aiding in our ability to pursue academic completion. While we reported having a high sense of self-efficacy and opportunities for collective efficacy, each of us reported having significantly higher connections to God/religious based problem solving and faith manifestations when considering ways to persist in our doctoral programs. Additionally, we shared a strong value placed on the importance of having a broad ranging (academic, professional, personal, and spiritual) community of support to successfully complete our programs. Several of the participants spoke specifically of the importance of establishing formal and informal cohorts with other peers of color in the program as an additional level of accountability and support to complete our programs. An interesting finding in the study was the relationship self-efficacy and faith manifestation had on the impact of self-doubt. Despite our strong sense of self-efficacy, when we spoke of our battles with self-doubt, we acknowledged our academic ability but that did not seem to assuage our self-doubt. However, when we talked about our faith and our belief and trust in God, we saw our self-doubt as no longer being a valid academic barrier. In fact, we saw self-doubt as a distraction from the goal of completion and felt empowered to move beyond our doubt. It is believed that this sense of empowerment is a consequence of the messages of hope and perseverance embedded in Christian theology. Each woman alluded to this belief that regardless of how difficult our academic experiences may have been, we were confident that God was with us on the journey and that we would overcome the challenges if we forged ahead. As stated by several of the participants, God provided consistent moments of confirmation and validation that we were on the right path in our programs, so it reinforced our belief that we would successfully complete our degrees. Based on the data, it appears this sense of empowerment was enough to mediate our battles with self-doubt.

From this circle of women sharing the ups and downs of our joys, pains, worries, disappointments, countless missteps, isolation, social and familial disconnection, accomplishments, multiple life events like births, deaths, and celebrations, I realized a pattern for goal completion emerged. Not only did we all personally experience and witness God's guidance and support in the Waiting Room, but I also discovered one of the key reasons for the purpose of my long eleven-year journey through the Waiting Room. In the discovery of my own resilience and persistence, God gifted me with practical tools to be shared with others going through their own goal-attainment Waiting Rooms. I termed this collection of tips, the "Five P's for Goal Completion". I am sharing these 5 key tactics with you in a way that is plainly spoken so they have the deep reaching impact for you as they had for me during my journey. The **5 P's** are:

1. Purpose – What is your vision? Be clear about what you want and why! This is the calling God placed on your heart. The long-held dream you have wanted to pursue. The passion project you have delayed pursuing for years. This is the secretly held hope that you have finally decided to step out on faith to make it happen. Write this in <u>**pen**</u> because this is significant and real!

2. Planning – What are the steps you need to take to make the vision a reality? Write this in PENCIL because this requires extreme flexibility. This is the journey work, so it ebbs and flows. This is the space where you get to have flexible faith in that you do not stop believing in God's ability to get you through the Waiting Room as the "stuff of life; the Job Moments" hit you from the left and right on an hourly, daily, weekly, monthly, annual basis. The purpose does not necessarily have to change (although the degree type and institution changed for me), but the plan will need to shift multiple times to get to the vision.

This is a difficult part of the journey. I started my academic journey when my son was about 3-3.5 years old. During my first academic program, I would leave him to travel to the West Coast for a week-long residential intensive each semester. I missed his graduation from kindergarten to first grade. I cried desperately, knowing that I was placing my dream above my heart's desire to celebrate his educational milestones. My mother, sisters, and his godfathers stood for him so I could forge on with my dream of becoming Dr. Keima Sheriff. I missed going out with friends for regular get-togethers and to celebrate major milestones. When the nation entered a recession, I went from making close to $90,000 a year to making $20,000. I had a mortgage that I entered in President Obama's mortgage relief program to save my home from foreclosure. My mother, who always said she never made it as far as I did academically but she would always be able to feed me, served as a major source of meals for me and my son. While in the second academic program, I was diagnosed with spinal arthritis that was immensely painful. Writing requires long hours of sitting which only exacerbates the arthritis. Each of these realities required planning, replanning, and sometimes scrapping all the plans and starting from scratch. Each time I thought I had a handle on the newest issue, another one appeared. Each version of the plan to get to the vision required my faith to be just as flexible as the plan. It was understanding that these challenges were not reasons to give up on the vision, but instead, to turn to God in deeper ways to see the new solution He was providing to address that specific issue. Use your pencil, embrace using the eraser (often), and keep the point sharp for the new plan!

3. Perspective – This is the mindset you will need to embrace to keep your mind focused on achieving the vision. You will make mistakes and have setbacks. Use them as amazing steppingstones to get closer to the Purpose, the vision! It's appreciating that each mistake is an opportunity for growth. Having a growth mindset will guard you against negatively internalizing feedback. This tactic was vitally important when it came to overcoming a two-and-a-half year writing paralysis because I negatively internalized a piece of critical feedback from my academic advisor from my first academic program. One day, when reviewing a paper, she said, "I had a wonderfully lyrical writing voice but needed to develop a stronger, dispassionate academic writing voice." I heard, "you can't write worth a damn and we have figured out that you are a fraud." I did not realize it then, but later reflection revealed that, negatively internalizing her critical feedback, sparked by a battle with imposter syndrome. Every time I attempted to write, the words escaped me. Always called an eloquent and inspiring speaker, I lost my ability to articulate my thoughts powerfully and convincingly. I suffered in deafening silence and deep pain. For 2.5 years I made up reasons about why I was not "done yet with my dissertation" when doctoral peers and non-academic family and friends would innocently inquire about my status. Often hearing, "Keima, you're an amazing writer and speaker, this paper is nothing you can't handle"; guilt, frustration, embarrassment, and depression would drill down deeper into my spirit with each passing inquiry. It was the blessing of several conversations with my sisters, mother, Pastor, work supervisor and most importantly, God, that pulled me out of that mindset. It was understanding the power of both verbalized and internalized words. I started telling myself internally, in my journal and out loud to interrupt negative thoughts, that I am an amazing writer who gets to expand my writing capacity. That I have something worthy to be said and would find a way to authentically say it while meeting the standards of academia. Shifting to a growth mindset allowed me to embrace mistakes and critical feedback as opportunities to expand. I went from seeing myself as an undeserving student to a theorist.

4. Persistence – Welcome to the Waiting Room! You will get tired, want to walk away, be frustrated, be forced to make sacrifices, doubt yourself and feel unable to meet the demands of the goal. This is when you may embrace thoughts that are actually not your own, but that of the enemy about your inability to achieve the dream. This is when you will need to hold captive and rebuke all negative thoughts and cast them straight to the pit of hell! This is when you need to dig in to achieve the purpose, the vision, your why, and accept that you will be successful! This was going to my professor at my second institution to humbly say, "on Friday my husband assaulted me because he did not want me to discover that his infidelity since right before we married never ended and in fact, he was with many more women than I knew. Unfortunately, I had to spend the weekend dealing with his arrest, filing a protection from abuse order for his first and only assault against me, and supporting my son with emotionally processing violence he had never witnessed before in his life. I am sorry I just did not have the brain space to get the final assignment done but if you give me an extension, I will get it done!" Had I not done the work on my mindset, I would not have been able to humble myself to ask for additional time to complete my assignment. After accepting that I was worthy of this dream, worthy of becoming Dr. Sheriff, I was unwilling to hold all of the "stuff" in anymore. I needed to be honest about what was happening in my life, ask for what I needed and fight for what I believed God had for me. If I needed more time because of a life barrier, I asked for it. If I could not do something because I needed to prioritize school, I declined the request or experience. As a morning person, I changed my life around, so that I started my weekdays at 3am to write before I had to get my son up for school. Weekends and Sundays after church became dedicated writing days. I asked my sisters and mother to watch my son, so I could stay after work for several hours to write. I wrote every day, even if it just meant working on the references, editing what I already wrote, or capturing random thoughts. The goal was to write, write, and write to stave off the desire to be perfect because a done dissertation is the Best dissertation!

5. Peace – This is the most powerful **P**! This is the way you persist, the way you develop the necessary perspective, how you will have the strength to plan and replan to arrive at the goal that is prayerfully aligned with God's will for your life. This is where you develop a grounding, centering, spiritual practice that allows you to stay engaged, positive, and restores your energy during the tough patches. This is when you talk to God and tell him all about your troubles! Every morning, I would get up, read the Daily Bread for the daily affirmation, read the scripture attached to the message and write out my prayers in my prayer journal. I went to bible study on Wednesday nights to hear what God had to say about my situation. I attended Saturday group prayer meetings to raise my voice with others because the Word says, "where two or more are gathered in my name, there am I with them (Holy Bible, 2011)".

I went to service weekly and laid my burdens at the altar for God to work out for me. I found ways to be of service to others whether in the church, community, at work or in my family. I participated in a leadership development course that focused on universal, spiritual truths. I searched for God while in my Waiting Room and found Him. Each time a new problem surfaced, I dug in deeper. Each time I felt myself succumbing to doubt, I dug in deeper. Each time I wondered if I would ever get to the finish line, I dug in deeper. Each time, each time, each time, I turned to God!

On November 15, 2018, I defended my research and successfully passed, becoming Dr. Keima N. Sheriff. Praise God! I want to encourage you to internalize the 5 P's! Live them! Allow them to be the points you reflect on every day to make sure that you are still on the path to accomplishing your goals despite whatever you may be feeling or thinking or what may be happening around you that feels completely out of your control. Let me remind you that you are capable. You made it this far in life so there ya go! You have a 100% batting average of overcoming challenges because you have made it this far. So there ya go! You have figured out how to stand tall when others have wanted you to stay knocked down. So there ya go! You have fought for the life you wanted and believed you could have despite the family and community stories you come from. So there ya go! You have figured out how to turn that little bit into a lot to survive yet another day. So there ya go! You have made up your mind to achieve your goal and that you will because you have a 100% batting average in surviving the stuff of life!

Five Tips while in The Waiting Room

1. Define your purpose!
2. Be clear (and flexible) with your plans to achieve your purpose!
3. Get your mindset together to determine what perspective - fixed or growth - you will have as you encounter the stuff of life!
4. Determine in your mind, body and spirit now that you will persist no matter what life throws at you!
5. Each day will bring its own opportunities and tasks, how will you find peace to deal with the business of the day!

Do this mental check every day and you will realize you will have so many more successfully completed days you have deposited into your life bank that you can rely on to get you closer and closer to your dreams! And always remember, the Waiting Room is the place where God is working on you as He prepares you for the dream, so the delay is not a denial. Just keep embracing each phase of the journey and you will see how He has prepared you for the blessing of the dream!

Peace,

Dr. Kem

Acknowledgements

Before I thank anyone else, I want to offer my deepest gratitude to God. Had I not gone through the Waiting Room of my doctoral journey, I would not have had an opportunity to witness to others going through their own journey. You empowered me to nurture the dream of becoming Dr. Keima Sheriff, no matter what experiences I encountered along the way. You stood beside me during my darkest days, carried me when I was convinced I could not move another step towards completion, and provided me with every necessary resource at the perfect time. God, I thank you for this opportunity to be an expression of your unyielding favor in the lives of your children to encourage all those who feel stuck, lost, forgotten, and ready to walk away from our dreams.

I want to thank Drs. Nicole Henderson and Adriene Hobdy. Both of you, in independent conversations, encouraged me to follow my dream of becoming an author. Nicole, thank you for introducing me to Debbie and this writing project.

I want to thank my son Sebelah, and my sisters, Yattah and Whedai, for checking in on me, encouraging me, and just being there for me. We are all going through a difficult time as we support Mommy through her transition from this life. The depression of spirit and ability to produce when faced with losing your parent is indescribable.

Mommy, you have been my everything. I have stood on your shoulders from the day you birthed me till the day I said, "Mommy." Please finally stand on mine as you lay in your hospice bed. I fought through the profound sadness of losing you to produce this chapter to be a blessing to others in the struggle. Thank you for giving me this amazing life Marie Blanton!

It is done....

Dedication

To my Mommy, Marie Blanton... The woman with amazing dreams that sacrificed for her children to live into theirs. How I wish you had more time. My love for you always!

Reflections

Reflections

_____

_____

_____

_____

_____

_____

_____

_____

_____

_____

_____

_____

_____

_____

_____

_____

_____

_____

_____

_____

_____

Reflections

VI

WAITING FOR
My Fairy Tale

EARLINA KING

I am Earlina Davis (Birth name means something to me). Originally from Greenville, North Carolina, I now reside in Virginia Beach, VA. I am very passionate about being where I am needed. I spent many years traveling up and through the DMV as a Court Reporter, certified in Conflict Resolution. I am a mother of three beautiful children: Antonio, Alani, and Roque. I enjoy spending time with my children and my friends. I am forever on a mission to change lives. When not working you will see me with my worship flags. I am a proud Praise Dance Minister.

As young girls,

we sometimes grow up with an idea of a fairytale life in our heads. I watched nothing but fairy tales growing up. You know, the stories that make life look perfect and have you thinking that all your dreams will come true, that one day your Prince Charming will come to your rescue, allowing you to live happily ever after. Do you all remember Cinderella? Her dad died and she had to live with her stepmother and two step-sisters. She was immediately the outsider and made to feel like she was not a part of the family. She could not do anything with them, including going to the ball with Prince Charming. We know that she was beautiful, she snuck off to the ball and danced the night away with this handsome man. He was captivated by her and she quickly disappeared; but not without losing her shoe. Eventually, Prince Charming looked for her, he found her and he married her not knowing much about her. I always wondered if Cinderella experienced a lifetime of trauma growing up; would he still have ridden off into the sunset with her? Think about it: her dad died; she was continually mistreated by those who were supposed to love her, and she was completely broken! Yet she still said, "I do!" She said it without healing from feeling like an outsider. She said it as a broken woman. She said, "I do!" feeling more like a liability. Whew, that was a lot!

Now that I am older I look at that movie very differently. You see, when I said, "I do!" it ushered me into the Waiting Room. Why? Well, my Prince

Charming was going to find me and I was going to be complete. I was going to be healed and all of the past wiped away. All of the trauma of my youth, and all the misplaced feelings would magically disappear when I got married and we rode off into the sunset, right? Saying those two words would change all the horrible things that happened to me. However, all the broken pieces from my childhood full of rejection and doubt were right beside me as I walked down the aisle. Did I feel it? Oh yes! With every step I took, I ignored it all and still said, "I do!"

I entered the Waiting Room and took a seat to wait for my soon-to-be fairytale to appear. I sat there believing nothing was going to stop it! I sat there waiting for when my Prince Charming would arrive. I sat there waiting to ride off into the sunset and my life would change forever. I knew that I would not have to figure it out. The adult in me turned into the little girl who was waiting. **Waiting** for the fairytale to appear. It never did.

If I can title my upbringing, it would be *The Unknown*. I was always trying to figure out what was next. Where was I going to sleep? Where will my next meal come from? What was my next adventure in life? I was always faced with figuring out how to grow from the seeds of womanhood that were never watered by who I wanted. About six months before my marriage, I was faced with so much uncertainty. I had absolutely **no** stability in my life. How was I going to be a confident woman, a wife, and a mom without ever having the proper classes? I did not have the upbringing or anyone to show me the way out of the waiting room from being a girl and becoming a woman. You know, if a seed is watered properly it grows. As a child, any experience that waters the seeds of your childhood can shape how you grow into adulthood. Let me explain my upbringing so this makes sense.

In the first chapter of my life, *The Unknown*, I grew up waiting–waiting to figure out what to do next. My life wasn't what you'd call a normal childhood, but to me it was normal. Only as I got older, I came to realize and understand that it really was anything but normal. My fairytale included picture-perfect parents, a big house for me and my siblings, and a dog. My reality was that my dad was not in the picture, although I knew of him and did get to meet him. (That's a story for another time.) And my mom was a single mom who worked *all* the time to support us. I wanted my mom to be happy, so I hated to see her exhausted and worn out. Although I was a child myself, I tried to help my sisters and brothers. We had a big family, so I pulled a lot of weight being the oldest girl. Being the oldest girl carried lots of responsibilities. While most teen years are filled with hobbies, sports, and sleepovers with friends, mine consisted of keeping my siblings together.We made the most of what we call good times. We were close. My mother tried her best to keep us together. She made such a huge imprint on my heart that no one has been able to fill. Even when I was no longer near her.

I can still vividly recall the rush of emotions on the day that all seven of us siblings were separated and placed into foster care. I could not understand why. I thought being a good child and helping around the house as much as possible meant this would never happen. Imagine for a moment the deep emotional pain and turmoil felt being separated from your only parent and siblings. Where was I going to sleep? Where would my next meal come

from? Was I ready for the next life adventure? Ugh! Here I was waiting–
waiting to see what would happen next. Waiting for my new living location
and new family, made me feel incomplete. There were no more good night
kisses, or "I love you my only red baby", as my mom would call me. I had no
control. I could only wait and wonder who was going to help me figure out
my life... who would I become?

The lady that took me in was loving and heavy into the church, which
was all foreign to me. Going to church on Sundays, listening to the choir,
watching everyone praise and be thankful. It was difficult to enjoy this
experience because it was so new to me. I had to quickly figure out this
newness. So, I blocked out a lot of my childhood and buried experiences
with my siblings so far down that I stopped hoping we would reconnect. I
decided to begin enjoying my new family while adapting to my new routines.
Yet, no matter how I tried to fill my time, I often wondered when my mom
was coming to get me. I just knew she'd be knocking on the door to pick
me up with kisses and hugs. How was this fairytale going to end? Would my
childhood seed ever be watered again by my mother?

In the fifth grade, the waiting was over and I was finally reunited with my
mom and siblings. The hugs and laughter were back. Parts of my fairytale
were restored and the waiting for my mother's water was over. In the short
time I was in the "waters of foster care" I grew in my patience and endurance.
I learned how to please others. I loved seeing others smile and experience
joy. I learned that it wasn't about me being happy, but about making others
happy. However, that lesson led to other *unknown* unfavorable adventures.

From middle school to high school, I continued to blindly wait on whatever would come my way next. This wasn't a healthy way to live but that's just the way the waters flowed with my family. By my Senior year, I had started dating. I wasn't seeking love but rather blocking out distractions and guarding my heart. My mom's guidance was that guys just wanted sex and I was not giving up my goodies!! That kept me waiting for that perfect someone. I still wanted the fairytale of true love. See as a Senior, while others were enjoying their last year of school, I was focused on working. On graduation day, I remember a news reporter following me, so I could share my story of living in a hotel while attending high school. I felt so insecure and afraid of who would know, what people would think, and why this was happening to us. I felt like the only seeds being planted in my life were negative and I never wanted to feel that feeling ever again, from anyone. Where was my Prince Charming to take me from this life? I was a pretty girl so I stood out, but my personality allowed me to master the art of blending in. I now understand that it's hard to identify seeds of love and healthy relationships when that wasn't your past life, nor were they sown into me.

As a young adult and high school graduate, life taught me that nothing was permanent and that at any time, things could be taken away from you. I also learned that in life and relationships, you have to grow up quickly. I had met some men who were not always law-abiding. Just as fast as they became my love partners, they got locked up from living the street life. Once again, I was rejected and alone. I waited and believed that I would have a better life. I just needed the right partner to stick with and the fairy tale life would then come true.

I wanted the important people in my life to be there with and for me. My father was one of them. I believed and knew he wanted to see me, although our visits were few and far in between. But when they did happen, I remember having a good time. My fairytale of having dad around ended with him dying and I took it so hard! I remember feeling and wishing I had more time with him so I blocked those painful feelings because in my mind if I didn't think about it, it could still happen. I was determined to have it all: the family, the relationship, and the life. This would be the beginning of the next chapter in my life's story, **The Unknown**.

I desperately desired to live a fairy tale life with the ideal family, ideal relationships, and an ideal life. I believed that if my fairytale would come true then all my troubles and emotional pain would disappear. Just like that! Oh, why did I think I'd find my fairytale partner in a nightclub? Who knows, but that's where I started frequenting. One night a good friend and I got dressed up and attended a nightclub. We rode around forever, looking for a good parking spot and upon exiting the car, these guys handed us a flyer. The flyer was to attend a party the next day in a mansion!! OMG! I just knew my Prince was in the mansion. We were so excited! The next day we attended the party at the mansion and when we walked in I saw the most handsome man. Is this him? Have I met Prince Charming? The house was huge; the music was great; I was feeling good. I knew at that moment I was either high off the ecstasy I had taken, or I met a guy that could be my everything. Turns out, I was high off Ecstasy pills…

The evening felt perfect and I was being treated like a princess. My Prince and I rode in his convertible with the wind blowing in my hair. The walk on the beach from his house was all so perfect. I felt so at peace and complete. Could I finally just rest from all the instabilities that I had going on in my life? Unfortunately, the drugs and partying caught up to me, and the next day I got sick. My Prince Charming took such great care of me by bathing me and allowing me to lay in his bed. Soon I began feeling like he was my prince, especially since he wanted me to be "the special one" to oversee the parties at the mansion. Often celebrities came to the house and I was the one to make sure that over 40 strippers were there to entertain everyone. He also made sure I looked the part with the hottest clothes, shoes, jewelry, and best food from only upscale restaurants. I felt like I was living in a reality TV show and I was the head lady in charge. I had become a real Princess and we even took amazing road trips together. I wanted to just embrace this new life and be done with anything of my past. I wanted to be Cinderella. I just wanted to live my life and not think of anything else. I wanted to ignore my past hurts and my childhood, but everything I was trying to suppress eventually came back full force. I couldn't run from the hurt. Something was still missing from my life and now I had to figure it out. I'm thankful God was listening to my heart.

RETURNING TO MY FIRST LOVE

One day a coworker invited me to church, which was odd because while I did not care for this woman, my spirit was drawn to her. I honestly missed the connection to the church that I experienced with my foster family. I chuckle now as I remember my foster family introducing me to church and Christ's love. I tried my best to forget the learning and love of Christ, but it didn't work. God was trying to give me what I was seeking, I just didn't know it at the time. With my foster family, I had gotten saved but had no spiritual foundation or stability. This is why it was easy to return to what I knew, partying. By this time I had a son. It was bigger than me. I had a baby that relied on me. Having a child forced me to grow up. He became the reason I existed. I still had questions about my life. Why did God choose me to be a parent? Why am I raising him alone? Am I a single mother due to my bad decisions? I was in a cycle of mental confusion. I had no order in my life and nothing was satisfying me. The partying, drugs, and drinking came to a halt. I still had male friends but I didn't believe anyone would be in my life permanently. I didn't believe I deserved love, so I accepted the toxic and unsteady behavior of my guy friends. The ones that I believed were in love with me I just pushed away.

I turned to the one I knew would permanently love me. I finally returned to my first love–Christ. Christ was the only one who proved to be a constant in my life. I rededicated my life to God. Finally, my topsy turvy world felt right but I still wanted love in human form. I was fixated on being married. I was determined to figure this thing out. I thought marriage would make up for the hurts I caused and the pain I inflicted on myself. My desire to complete my family was so strong that I ignored the fact that I needed healing. The trauma of my childhood altered me so badly that if I could just lock in a partner, it would all go away. My life was out of control. In haste, I accepted a new career, as a Court Reporter. They offered to pay me to relocate to Roanoke, Virginia. I thought it was a power move, so without seeking wise counsel, I left the little stability I had.

I was now focused on working and my past was a distant memory. I now had two children. Without the influence of drugs, I thought my daughter's father could be my Prince Charming. I kept looking for a man's presence to fill my void. I started attending church and one Sunday the Pastor asked, "Do you know God?" As I sat with that question lingering, my life decisions began flashing before me. I understood that I wanted the fairy tale so badly that I was overlooking the red flags in my relationship. Why did I think marriage was the magic pill to cure everything? Here's the kicker. The red flags were coming from me. I needed to be addressed. All this time, I was setting myself up for failure just so I could portray an image to my friends, family, and yes, even the church.

Red flags didn't stop me. Planning a wedding had me living in the fairytale of glitz and glam. The bridal showers and family gatherings would lead to marriage and all the sex I wanted! All judgments about me would be gone and I'll live happily ever after. I imagined marriage to be where I would find myself, satisfy my husband, and pour into my children because this was never done for me. Marriage was going to be about having parties, traveling with other couples, going on girl's trips, having amazing intimacy, and feeling like I had become the Queen and the envy of the kingdom. Foolishness!

The wedding was over and I waited and waited for this amazing life. I stared out of the window and thought about how I'd lost myself completely. I stopped hanging out with friends and self-care went out the window. I did not want to draw attention to myself. The waiting room was calling me again. I was supposed to be Cinderella, but instead, life was a nightmare!

I put myself into a Waiting Room because I was waiting for an illusion to be my reality. I didn't understand that I needed to work on myself first before I could give myself to anyone else. I accepted a lower standard in relationships because of my low self-worth. I was waiting for this magical feeling to overtake me. You see, just like Cinderella I had the worst deal in life. Like her, I poured my heart out and did whatever it took to earn acceptance and love. I thought I found it and Prince Charming would sweep me off my feet. The story says she lived happily ever after. But did she?

How could Cinderella possibly live happily ever after with no healing? When did she work through her trauma?

RELEASE

God has a way of redirecting us and that is exactly what He did for me. From the outside, it seemed that I had it all together–my children were great, we had fun family outings, and I had a good job. But what about the inner turmoil? Where's the concern for my mental health? What about my mental peace? When will my traumatic life events be addressed? What about that rejection I felt growing up? How do I learn to trust? How do I learn my worth? All of this should have been addressed before my marriage. Wives, whether you have been married one day or 50 years, understand yourselves first. Trying to show that you have a perfect life can make you dizzy. Your imperfections *will* begin to seep through. I've been married for 10 years and I finally understand what a wife is.

My advice is to make sure you are mentally healed and complete before walking down the aisle. Do not rush to get down the aisle until you understand your partner's true intentions. Having learned these things in hindsight had me walking towards the exit of my marriage. I learned through a dream that everything I needed to be happy was already inside me and did not come from another person. After exploring this more, I had to acknowledge that I needed God's help and professional help. I cannot rewrite my childhood but I can learn to live with it. With the help of an amazing therapist, I'm now able to go back in time and speak about/relive those experiences that I swore I'd never speak about again. I needed to heal those wounds. I had to face my experiences and begin understanding myself. Once I did that, it put a lot of things into perspective and explained why I functioned the way I did.

My self-esteem got better. My self-worth increased. Growth came from therapy. I am now a better person, a better wife, a better mom, and a better friend. Doing the work while I was in the Waiting Room led to seeing my internal beauty.

What are the strategies that helped me? These are the main seeds I had to re-water:

1. **Asking God to search me and help me.** It was not easy. A daily walk of denying myself. I cried many days while shedding old behaviors and trying not to respond to trigger words. Loving myself and loving others as Christ would want me to was another task. I realized that I needed quiet time to just sit and let God speak to me. Addressing some hurts from my past and dealing with them was hard, and there were days I didn't think I could do it. Yet, God kept me, and if you are reading this, He is keeping you too. My eyes became open to people around me that needed to be moved and God showed me they should've never been in my circle to begin with. People-pleasing Earlina was now gone.

2. **Fasting and seeking God's help.** I learned to shed healthy tears and stop internalizing my feelings. I was taught as a child to be seen and only speak when spoken to. That lingered until adulthood. I had to learn to express my thoughts and feelings. I had to identify those triggers that prompted me to get out of character. I created boundaries and prioritized myself. It's okay to beautify yourself. I practice self-care and do what makes me feel good.

3. **Releasing and moving on.** Another lesson I learned as a child was to make sure that I left things operable, just like I found them. I had to learn to stop wanting to fix people. God had to really deal with me in this area. I've learned that sometimes my only job is to plant and release. Through fasting and reading the Word, along with spending time with God, I'm much better. Releasing is healing too. God came

in and made me whole when I let go and opened a way for him to enter. Please consider this before saying I do. Hopefully, Cinderella completed her steps of healing at some point after saying, "I do."

In closing, there are some wrongs that you just have to let go of. Have faith and believe Jesus died on the cross for our sins. Ask God to search you and show you the things you thought you released and healed from. I love God for not counting it robbery to come to my aid. God knows I took doubt down the aisle. I walked into marriage believing that it wouldn't work because of my past and upbringing. Nothing lasts forever, right? If this is you, there is a good chance you may need to wait before saying, "I do."

Nonetheless, I *still* believe that marriage is a beautiful part of life God provided to us. It is indeed for better or worse, but please resolve issues needing to be addressed before committing. Getting out of the Waiting Room took years. It is a journey, but you **will come out** better. Before you say 'Yes' be complete, know yourself, and heal first. Prince Charming will find you. He will bring you to balance, your morals and values will align and you will not have to convince him about God and God's light. Better yet, your Prince Charming will stand with you as you walk out of the Waiting Room.

Five Tips while in The Waiting Room

1. If you have a relationship with God, talk and ask Him for guidance on your next steps. Speak to HIm from your heart in plain language. Believe me, if you're at this point in The Waiting Room, God has probably already been speaking and now it is your turn to move.

2. Stop in your tracks if you think saying I Do is going to fix your life. Don't make the same mistake I made. Use my example to save yourself some heartache.

3. Seek counseling if needed. Your mental health is important. You are not a superwoman.

4. If you are already married, do what's needed for you. Embrace your place in life but focus on self-care. Women spend countless hours working and taking care of everyone else, and sometimes we lose ourselves in the process. It's okay to have me-time. Little by little, you will start to find yourself again.

5. If you don't take anything else from my chapter, take away this: Truth. The Holy Spirit will lead you to the truth of yourself, of others, of where you are currently, and where you need to be. The Waiting Room is a process that will lead you to being whole and complete.

Acknowledgments

First and foremost I have to thank God for the guidance of the Holy Spirit and for never leaving me. God has aligned several key people to drop into my life, and without them or Him, I'm not sure where I'd be.

I want to say thank you to my three children. They pushed me to better myself and to stop waiting. Thank you for urging me to get out of the Waiting Room before it was too late.

Dedication

I dedicate this chapter to the women that are in a waiting season trying to find themselves before or after saying I do. If this just reaches one lady who decides that she needs to learn and love herself first, and that marriage does not complete her, then my job is done. Healing from childhood trauma has to take place, hopefully before wedding vows, but if not, know that it's never too late to find you again!

This chapter is dedicated to the woman who is tired and anxious and ready to fix herself and her life!

Reflections

_____
_____
_____
_____
_____
_____
_____
_____
_____
_____
_____
_____
_____
_____
_____
_____
_____
_____
_____
_____

Reflections

Final Words from The Visionary...

I couldn't let this book close without gifting you with words from me. Here goes, you ready? Just cuz' you are currently out of The Waiting Room, doesn't mean you won't return soon. Let that marinate.

The Waiting Room is Cyclical!

I feel like I'm constantly in The Waiting Room. Waiting for my dad to be a father & fully acknowledge me. Waiting for my family to understand that drugs is slowly taking us out. Waiting for my family to reconnect since Grandma passed away. Waiting to get financially free after filing bankruptcy. Waiting for love after my second divorce. Waiting for the dream job to call me after being laid off twice. Waiting for the easy button to appear since becoming an entrepreneur! Waiting for life to get easier since saying YES to walking in my purpose.

Maybe it's just me who spends countless hours in The Waiting Room. Waiting to get to the other side of "this" issue. Your issue may look different from mine, but we are all waiting. So why write this book? What makes the waiting different this time? For me, it's because I know GOD has a plan for my life. This wait was in HIS plans. Sometimes it takes a while for GOD to orchestrate things in our lives.

But while you're waiting, what's your attitude? See me, I'm impatient, but GOD knows this because HE designed me. I feel like I'm often in The Waiting Room because GOD is working on my attitude. See this last wait was different? I decided in December to aggressively find full-time employment after being an authorpreneur for 3 years. I understood that I can walk in my purpose AND work full-time. I just knew with my degrees and years of experience, finding a job would be a cake walk. LIES! It took me five grueling months to land a job. But not just any job. It was one that I prayed for with all the perks I asked GOD for. HE delivered, but baby, that five months was humbling. GOD helped me realize quickly that I am NOTHING without him. He got my attitude all the way together.

Five months in The Waiting Room. What did my days look like? Prayer, tears of frustration, repentance for not trusting GOD fully, humiliation after receiving reject notice after reject notice, doubt, fear and more. Every time I caught myself sabotaging my prayers or filled with doubt, I found a reason to say Thank You. Whether it was cheering on friends who seemed to be getting their prayers answered quicker than mine, or finding women on Social Media that I could support and encourage, or just sitting in gratitude with my devotional. I understood that I needed to say Thank You in advance of my blessing. That was my attitude adjustment.

Then I had to work on my why? Why did I want a job? Was I not trusting GOD to provide? What will I do with this blessing? See, it was important to me that I continue to work on the things GOD told me to: writing books and working with women. I suffered with anxiety when I became an authorpreneur.

My money was funny some days, couldn't do what I wanted financially, but again I had to press pause. For 3 years as a full-time self-employed woman, not ONE thing was missing from my life. My needs were met. Again, I had to say Thank You.

So we addressed the attitude and the intent. The final thing for me was my worship. I had to learn to worship GOD as if the door had already been opened. I needed to kick it up a notch. Now, worship is personal. I'm not a shouter but I sing and feel worship songs until I'm in tears. I'd sit in worship and speak my blessing and GOD's promises over and over until my face was drenched. That was my worship.

Sis, you've got to find your voice. Say what it is you're waiting for! Why is it important and how can it be used to increase GOD's kingdom? Will you worship while you wait? Will you clap for other women when you see GOD blessing them?

The Waiting Room can be intimidating, but sis, when you get that blessing you've been waiting for!! Baby, that moment when you know that GOD has been listening to every prayer and with you in The Waiting Room the ENTIRE time! There's power in your prayers.. Now excuse me, I gotta run and tell someone else about how good GOD has been to me!!

Debbie